THE PAINTER PAINTS AWAY THE DAY

(A civil servant remembers)

RAKESH AGARWAL

BLUEROSE PUBLISHERS
India | U.K.

Copyright © Rakesh Agarwal 2024

All rights reserved by author. No part of this publication may be reproduced, stored in a retrieval system or transmitted in any form or by any means, electronic, mechanical, photocopying, recording or otherwise, without the prior permission of the author. Although every precaution has been taken to verify the accuracy of the information contained herein, the publisher assumes no responsibility for any errors or omissions. No liability is assumed for damages that may result from the use of information contained within.

BlueRose Publishers takes no responsibility for any damages, losses, or liabilities that may arise from the use or misuse of the information, products, or services provided in this publication.

For permissions requests or inquiries regarding this publication, please contact:

BLUEROSE PUBLISHERS
www.BlueRoseONE.com
info@bluerosepublishers.com
+91 8882 898 898
+4407342408967

ISBN: 978-93-5989-167-5

Cover design: Shivam
Typesetting: Namrata Saini

First Edition: February 2024

My parents

Dedicated to my mother who passed away at the age of 83 years, at Allahabad.

And father who died at the age of 75 years.

And

To my wife, Nishi, and my son Siddhansh, who tirelessly helped me through the script.

Vincent van Gogh

<u>Inspiration of Paul Anka's "The Painter" on the tragic life of the Dutch painter Vincent Van Gogh</u>

The painter paints away the day
As he paints his life away
Will he rise in judgment's eye or fall.
What a humble life he leads
He never sees the price they give
Another part of his soul upon the wall.
like a lonely soldier faces,
Foreign shores of empty spaces
Such is he who strokes to free his soul

Isolation steeped in sadness
Mellowed by the fears of madness
There he stands as he commands control.

Deeper than the eye can see
Another man's philosophy
While he lives the price they give is small.

When he dies and on that day
The sky's high a price they'll pay
While he lives the price they give is small.

There was neither non-existence nor existence then; there was neither the realm of space nor the sky which is beyond. What stirred? Where? In whose protection?

Rig Veda

The origin of the universe is a mystery. There are no religious certitudes, no religious commands, no rituals. There is an emphasis on the need to probe and an invitation to discover one's own truth, **our uniqueness.**

The Setting

I was born in Allahabad, in a joint family.

I am told that I was born in Badshahi Mandi, an old area of Allahabad, in a humble setting. The midwife who delivered me was a formidable woman called Papa, the adorable midwife, adept at deliveries, was more reliable than doctors or hospitals. I was born on a hot summer day of 2nd June, 1956, delivered to the world by this woman from my mother's womb.

I was curious to see my earliest picture, if any. My Asha Mausi had taken a shot of me in the arms of my mother.

I was shocked. I looked like a small mouse with a big tail. I was very disturbed to see it – such an ugly child. Embarrassed, I asked my Bua why I had a tail. Her reassuring answer was that all new borns have a tail which slowly disappears. I checked my back and indeed there was no tail now. No-one told me that the supposed tail was the umbilical cord, which was cut later at the child's nave. I was ashamed of my ugly appearance.

I retired in 2016.This has since, given me a lot of time to think.

I am flooded by the memories of the past.

It was a quiet winter morning. I sat in my garden and enjoyed the mild sun and the light breeze. There was an embalming silence. Bird cries became more and more distant, as sleep overpowered me. I could faintly register the world around and slipped into a rabbit hole of memories.

From its labyrinthine pathways I pulled out the nuggets of memory one by one from the enchanted past.

Forgotten old pictures of people and places that mattered crowded the mind.

The earliest remembrance is that of Allahabad, the city of my birth.

Vintage old pictures of the city give an idea of the kind of city it was.

Akbar's fort on the bank of Yamuna, built in 1616, still standing strong.

Akbar fort
(Allahabad)

old bridge naini

The All Saints Cathedral, Allahabad

Highcourt Allahabad

The High Court of Ajudicature, at Allahabad, built by the Britishers in 1866

Chowk Allahabad

Allahabad Railway Station (1908)

mayo memorial hall (1879)

A.G. Office (old building)

Allahabad fort during kumbh (1928)

khushrobagh (19th century)

Contents

The City: It's Architecture and Culture 1

Festivals: celebrations in Allahabad 10

Seasons Changing seasons all the time bring disturbing and unsettling thoughts… 16

Some old pictures of the family which show our humble beginnings 23

Joint family from father's side 32

School Days 54

Early Postings 64

Overall reflections on Bureaucracy 78

Photography 88

Reading 89

Some travel memories that bring me back to my search for answers… 93

Portait of my mother 106

Some travel pictures 107

Hyderabad art exhibition 108

Bhutaan 110

The USA 116

Journey's end 121

The other explanation 123

Closing thoughts… 127

My Paintings: a glimpse 129

The City: It's Architecture and Culture

Allahabad, as I recollect, was a beautiful city with straight roads and planned grids of the British period. The Civil Lines area was a model of city planning – houses with acres of land surrounding them in well planned rectangles. Pace of life was slow and unhurried. There were lovely Gothic structures like All Saints' Cathedral, the Mayo Hall, the University, the High Court, the AG's office complex, the Minto Park, etc. These were not just utilitarian or functional buildings, but they embodied and spoke the language and culture of the British Colonial period. While they exuded the power of the Raj, they were also masterpieces of architecture, which we have even now, failed to replicate. The Alfred Park housed the statue of Queen Victoria, of course now removed.

Being an ancient pious city, the seat of religious activities is the confluence of Ganga and Yamuna. I remember fondly the great boat rides we took to the Sangam. The dip in the cool flowing waters, upto the chest height was fun. After the initial shock of cold immersion, we would jump and frolic for long hours. There were small sand outcrops/islands in the river and it was great fun to walk up to them. The water level was gone down considerably, only less than knee deep.

The need for hot food is accentuated after bath in the river. Delicious puris, aloo and baingan subzis were freshly prepared by the halwais on the ghat. Food was out of the world. The darshan of Bade Hanumanji was essential, after the 'snan' or river bath.

There is a huge idol of Lord Hanumanji, more than 20 feet in size, the only idol of Hanumanji in the country, which is in a lying posture, and washed every year by the Ganga in flood. Again, a revered place.

The bank of the river is dominated by the red fort, built by Akbar, and along the bank a boat ride along the Saraswati ghat, on the Yamuna, used to be beautiful and serene, with the slow rhythmic 'chop chop' of the oars of the boatsmen. One could loosen up an avalanche of happy thoughts from the past during the ride. In the moonlight, the ride became romantic as Sri Jaishankar Prasad, the Hindi poet, expressed in his immortal piece, 'Chandni raat mein nauka vihar'.

The city had a unique cultural heritage, absent in other KAVAL towns of Uttar Pradesh. The judges, the lawyers, the University professors and lecturers, the writers, all exuded their thoroughbred roots, a kind of rootedness.

My father had formed a Gita Society, whose members met once a week, to talk and discuss different chapters of the holy book. Justice ND Ojha, Justice Amitabh Banerji and Dr BL Agarwal were men of exceptional probity and learning. It was a pleasure to listen to their expositions on the Gita.

The city, less crowded, with huge open spaces was overladen with history. The pace was slow, langorous and its people were highly laid back. The heritage of Motilal Nehru, Jawaharlal Nehru, the Anand Bhawan, the literatteurs and writers like Harivansh Rai Bachchan, Firaq, Nirala, Mahadevi Verma, Ishwar Chand, etc seeped into the fabric of the town.

The Allahabad University boasts of massive Gothic towers, in a sprawling twin campus, one for the Science and the other for Arts department. Illustrious teachers adorned both the departments, known for their erudition and research. The alumni vouch for the academic standard of the institution, way ahead of other universities.

But now the rot has set in and can be seen everywhere – in the quality of teachers and the students both. Politics and selfishness has set in. The Academic Council discusses everything that is not academic.Entire academic years are lost in students' strike and the gheraos.

The adjoining Minto Park on the banks of the Yamuna, was a favourite picnic place. It was dominated by a gigantic monument of marble, in the memory of Lord Minto. In the cool moonlight it glistened like moonstone. Our picnic pack was opened here and to the joys of the game of antakshiri, we enjoyed a sumptuous meal. The 'Sangam Mahal' of the film 'Mahal' is near the Minto Park.

A galaxy of writers, poets and political doyens hail from the city– Mahadevi Verma, Jai Shankar Prasad, Nirala, Harivansh Rai Bachchan, Firaq Gorakhpuri, Pt Jawaharlal Nehru, Indira Gandhi, etc, all stalwarts in their fields. Allahabad boasts of and was truly the cultural and educational nerve centre of the country. Alumnis of the Allahabad University still adorn the top administrative posts in the country.

The Allahabad High Court of Judicature was one of the first, established by the British Government, way back in 1866. Some of the best legal luminaries, judges and lawyers trace their origin to the hallowed precincts of the High Court. The judges were an epitome of honesty and probity. They wore the wigs in the British times, which gave them a formidable appearance. Belonging to the legal family, I got to see them at close quarters.

The sprawling gardens surrounding the high court building, were a favourite place for morning walkers. We would often attack the luscious date trees with stones and partake of the fruits. The ripe pink jungle jalebis were another prize in summer months.

The age has passed. The precinct is unrecognizable now, crammed with the parked cars of judges and lawyers.

The Indian Coffee House is an institution by itself – the meeting place of politicians, writers, lawyers, etc, over cups of coffee and cigarettes. It is run by the

Kerala Cooperative Society. Service is available to get the dosas and coffee in the car itself. The cheese sandwiches used to be delectable. Many a rainy days were spent, in the coffee house, gorging the stuff, sitting in the comfort of our car.

Allahabad is still remembered for the delicious falooda kulfi from Loknath. Hari's desi ghee samosas were a gourmet's delight, still unsurpassed. They were so good, they could be preserved for a month without spoiling. Sulaki's sweets and kachories and aloo baingan ki bhaji still activate the saliva in the mouth. And the city served the best 'chat' to chat lovers. The wonderful aloo tikkis and pani phulki of Lal patthar chatwala in the chowk market are unbeatable. To top the fare, were the unparalleled paans of various shops in the city. Pan is traditionally eaten after both the meals in Allahabad. The stuff would melt in the mouth. Even non eaters become ardent fans.

The city hosts a stupendous Kumbh Mela on the banks of River Ganga, once every 12 years. It' s the biggest congregation of religious babas, gurus and New Age adepts. International coverage is given to the biggest fair in the world, spread in an area of about 10 to 20 square kilometres. Numerous pontoon bridges are built across the river for providing easy crossing to the devotees. The religious fervor reaches the highest pitch on 'nahan', the bathing days, when akharas after akharas of naked naga sadhus jumped and screamed in pleasure as they plunged into the river for the auspicious bath. Certain days are marked for attaining maximum 'punya'. Camps and tents are set up for a month long stay of the kalpvasis on the banks. Sadhus from all over the country, major 'maths' and ashrams took pride to participate. The devotees went on a boat to the confluene point of the Ganga and the Yamuna to take the holy dip and earn maximum 'punya'. The essence of the Hindu culture and fervor are on display. International spiritual seekers, writers and photographers cover the biggest international mela of the world, marveling at the congregation. Pravachans, religious books, artifacts like the rudrakshas, etc are available for the asking.

Kumbha Mela has become a spiritual marketplace. There are naked naga babas, performing feats on swings, some putting a fork through their penis, some lying on a bed of thorns, some in upturned posture. Droll and grotesque! A fascinating drama of the derelict spiritual life of the country! The good old simplicity of faith and the religious fervor of the gurus' and sadhus' camps is absent. There is an air of phoniness.

McPherson Lake was a big river front park, and a popular resort, in the cantonment area, with calm and serene winds and the Ganga waters. There were a lot of waterbirds, and acres of farms that grew mainly wheat. Crops undulated with the wind. It was actually a 'chandmari', for the target shooting practice of the jawans. But the serenity of the wind-swept landscape, in a back of beyond area of the city, attracts the quite a few sojourners, far from the madding crowd. We went for a picnic in a big party. The ground was overgrown with giant grass and crops. We had lost our way. The two parties, one led by Mamaji with children, and the other by Daya Mausiji with Mummy and other ladies lost each other.

In bewilderment, they shouted "Bhappu,' Bhappu," nickname for Mamaji. After an hour of cross search, we all met exhausted and frightened, tempers high. We all found each other hidden in the tall crops and grasses. We had sumptuous 'Chhole Bhature' of 'Chunni Lal' the famous shop in Civil Lines, to end the day.

Softy ice cream was newly introduced in the town, and it was available only at the Naini cafeteria, across the Yamuna bridge. People drove in troves to the novel haunt.

The Prayag Sangeet Samiti was the iconic cultural hub of the city. Top dancers, musicians and other cultural icons of the country hold their concerts here with pride. The kathak performance of Birju Maharaj and the tabla of Gudai Maharaj gripped the mesmerized audience. Danseuse like Hema Malini, Sitara Devi, Classical maestros like Pandit Jasraj, Kumar Gandharva, Begum Akhtar, Bhimsen Joshi and Ghulam Ali Khan prided themselves as regular performers.

Over the years, there has been a steady deterioration of the city. I went there almost as a ritual every year.

Gone are the massive spaces and gardens that surrounded the elegant residential houses in the civil lines area. Gone are the days of lazy shopping in the well-appointed shops in the civil lines. Now roads are crammed with innumerable tin-shed shops. The beautiful Ganga statue and the water fountain at the centre of the main market is no longer visible as it is hidden by the hoardings and posters. The chowk and other older parts of the city are so crowded that it is impossible to reach them by car.

The old-world flavour of Allahabad is captured in the verse below:

सुनव, मैं प्रयागराज़ हां.. हजारवां हजार रांग कलए

अकबर इलाहाबादी का इलाहाबाद हां.. किराक के शेरवां ,

'बच्चन की ककवताओं' और महादेवी की पीड़ा का एहसास हीँ..

सुनव, मै प्रयागराज हीँ..।

अपनी गवदी में छुपाए

लाखवां 'गुनाहवां के देवताओं ' का राज हीँ..

कमलेश्वर के 'ककतने पाककस्तान' का आगाज हां..

कनराला की 'शाखि पूजा' का 'राम' हां.. 'वह तवड़ती पत्थर' की गुरबत का एहसास हीँ.. सुनव, मैं प्रयागराज हीँ..। कवश्वकवद्यालय की गौरव गाथा का जीता जागता प्रमाण हीँ.. छात्वां के मन में पल रहे सपनवां की बुकनयाद हां..

प्राक्टर ऑकिस के बगल में आई कार्ड पाने के कलए लगे नव-आगांतुकवां कक कतार हां..

इांखिश कर्पाटडमेंट के कवने वाले कमरे में बैठे नवयुगल के मन का ख्वाब हीँ..

दशकवां पुराने बरगद की छांव में उस कवमल हाथवां के स्पशड का पकवत् भाव हीँ..

सुनव, मैं प्रयागराज हीँ..। हास्टलवां में दशकवां से पसरे मठाधीशवां का अलग ही सांसार हीँ..

छात् सांघ भवन से उठती छात् राजनीकत की हांकार हां..

कवकचांग में ि०ीस कम कराते छात् नेता का भौकाल हीँ..

मऊआइमा के बारूदवां से बने बमवां की आवाज हीँ..

सुनव, मैं प्रयागराज हीँ..।

सात पुश्तां कव तारने का भारी-भरकम बवझ कलए तेकलयरगांज, छवटा बघाड़ा, दारागांज, सलवरी, अल्लापुर, गवकवांदपुर के सुरांगनुमा कमरवां में रहने वाले प्रकतयवगी छात्वां के हौसला, कवश्वास और समपडण का भाव हीँ..

टूटते, कबखरते और सांवरते सपनवां का अद्भुत सांसार हां..

सुनव, मैं प्रयागराज हीँ..। मई जून की तपती दवपहरी में बैंक रवरू पर गन्ने के रस से तर हवते गले की शीतल प्यास हीँ..

यूकनवकसडटी रवरू के दवनवां तरि कबक रही ककताबवां में वेद, कुरआन, इकतहास, दशडन, घटना चक्र, ध्येय, दकि आकद का ज्ञान हीँ.. सुनव, मैं प्रयागराज हीँ..।

कटरा में नेतराम के शुद्ध घी वाली कचौड़ी और अल्लापुर में मुन्ना स्वीट की कमठाई, दारागांज में गुप्ता की चाय समवसे का स्वाद हीँ..

बैरहना का देहाती रसगुल्ला, चाट लाजवाब हीँ.. खवखा राय के दही बड़े का अद्भुत एहसास हीँ..

लवखनाथ में राजाराम की लस्सी, कनराला की चाट, हरर राम के समवसे, मातादीन की गजक, व टांर्न भैया के ऊन, कसकवल लाइन्स में हीरा हलवाई की दही जलेबी के साथ पुराने शहर की कबरयानी के जायके का अवणडनीय आस्वाद हीँ..

सुनव, मैं प्रयागराज हीँ..।

सम्राट अशवक के ककले कक प्राचीरवां से उठता कहांदुस्तान का स्वाकभमान हां..

अल्फ्रे रू पाकड में आजाद के कपस्टल से कनकलती गवकलयवां की आवाज हीँ.. देश के दुश्मनवां के कलए खौिः का पयाडय हीँ.. आनांद भवन से गूंजती राि‌रीय आंदवलन की ललकार हीँ.. सुनव, मैं प्रयागराज हीँ..। कांुः भ की अगाध श्रद्धा और कवश्वास हां.. लेटे हनुमान, नाग बासुकक का जागता हआ भखि भाव हीँ.. मनकामनेश्वर के चरणवां में बैठे भि की आस हीँ.. पत्थर कगरजाघर की खूबसूरती लाजवाब हीँ..

सि द मखिद, जामा मखिद और ऐसी ही अनेकवनेक मखिदवां से इबादत में उठता हआ हाथ हीँ.. लवकनाथ चौराहे पर कपड़ा ि◌ाड़ हवली का हड़दांग हीँ.. जॉनसनगांज के बुद्धा ताकजया का या हसैन बवल मुहम्मदी का आह्वान हीँ.. सुनव, मैं प्रयागराज हीँ..। खुसरव बाग के लाल अमरूद की कमठास हीँ.. सांगम की रेती पर हजारवां हजार साल से कलखता कमटाता इकतहास हीँ..

जांक्शन से गुजरती टरेनवां में बैठे राहगीरवां का इलाहाबाद कव एक बार किर से जी लेने का अधूरा सा ख्वाब हीँ.. सीनेट हाल की मीनार पर रुकी हई घड़ी के चलने का इांतजार हां..

सुनव, "मैं प्रयागराज हीँ"

(कै से बनता है इलाहाबादी ?)

ऐसा माना जाता है कक

पृथ्वी

अकि जल आकाश वायु

इन पांच तत्वां से मनुष्य बनता है और जब इसमें

यूकनवकसडटी रवर् की चाय सुलाकी की खस्ता-कचवरी दमआलू के साथ नेतराम के मवतीचूर के लर्॒र्॒ॢ लवकनाथ की रबड़ी मलाई देशी घी की जलेबी रबड़ी/या दही के साथ जगराम की देशी घी की बालूशाही खुशरूबाग के अमरुद सांगम का जल

बांधा वाले हनुमान जी का आशीष और आखखर में बुलाकी का पान कमलाया जाता है तब जा कर कही ि◌ॏॕएक कमबख्त "इलाहाबादी" बनता है.

Allahabad gave me the warmth of life.

Festivals: celebrations in Allahabad

Steeped in the religious and holy spirit, the city celebrates the major Hindu festivals in a unique manner, which brought joy to my childhood days.

Holi on the night of Holi, a 'holika' (the holy bonfire) is lighted. An intense fire grew up and reached the sky. Tamarind branches were stacked up, loaded with raw tamarind fruits. The heat of fire singed and burst them with a 'pop'. The taste of roasted tamarinds with black salt, ignited the gastric juices overtime.

THE carnival of colours began the next day. Unsuspecting cousins were rudely greeted with buckets of water thrown on them in the bed. It was unceremonious and unsparing.

We then collected outside in the warmth of the sun. There would be liberal sprinkling of colours on each other. The best and fastest of colours were purchased. Rama Chachi became the butt. Her sharp tongue made her the common target of the day, but she was alone enough to handle all.

We had full five happy hours of rocking time with the colours, both wet and dry. Gujhias, samosas and kanji, prepared in advance by my mother were liberally provided to the holi revelers. Bhang was laced in 'thandai' by Ramesh Chacha.

After it was over, to wash the colours from our bodies, and to prepare for the school next day, used to be an ordeal .

We then went to our Nanaji's place at Thornhill Road, for holi. What a ruckus was created, everyone shouting and running with pichkaris. Tanks and tubs of colours made out of palash flowers in lukewarm water were deliciously warm on our shivering bodies. The big cement tank in the courtyard would be the final destination for all. New members in the family were forcibly picked and thrown in. My Mamaji and Mausijis were old hands in the revelry. They took the lead. The spirit gripped us all. The smell of the saffron palash flowers, 'tesu', used to be heady in the warm water in which it was dissolved. The lukewarm water was embalming and soothing to shivering bodies, to say the least. Tesu does not hurt the eyes. The tank was like a hot spring, deliciously fragrant.

Mamaji was the supreme commander of the operations. Mamiji was mortally afraid of colours, but after a few remonstrations, she too would be dragged out from her hideout and attacked with 'pichkaris' and despatched to the water tank. Nishi too had to face the same treatment on her first holi. Later we were compulsorily feasted with the dose of 'bhang ka gola' in the 'thandai', a ritual practice in Allahabad.

Dussehra was a ten day extravaganza in the town.

We went to see all 'Ram dal' processions of different mohallas. The aesthetic taste and money spent on the tableaus, the themes based chosen from the epics, were awesome. Of all UP towns, Allahabad was known for the special way that Dussehra was celebrated.

The early morning, 4 am tableaus, were the last word in beauty, grandeur and artwork. We used to wake up with great enthusiasm every morning and were packed in a single car. The faithful old landmaster.

Lighting in the streets used to be exquisite. The festive spirit of the people was contagious. loudspeakers blared the Ramayana episodes by the singer Pandit Niranjan Sharma. The town throbbed with excitement. Ten major processions in ten mohallas were taken out every evening, one day for each mohalla. Fanfare and fervor came naturally to the residents. There were no Bajrang dals or RSS influence in those days. The religious spirit was spontaneous. Pajawa and Patharchatti were the two competing committees that organized the show.

For civil lines Ramdal, my cousin, Guddi was chosen to portray Lord Krishna, who sat on a crescent moon, and supplied saris from the moon to poor Draupadi who was being disrobed by the evil Duryodhana. Guddi had to suffer the onslaught of moths and mosquitos under the glare of the harsh mercury light.

But she bore it bravely.

For Katra Ramdal, we went to Naniji's sprawling bungalow at Katra, owners of lakshmi Talkies. We would sit on the boundary wall to watch the procession. Elders, leaning against the wall, would give a running commentary on the tableaus. We would munch peanuts and drop them on the unsuspecting policemen, below us. Poor 'mamus' would be taken by surprise and turned around to pin down the culprit. We of course, were the epitome of innocence in those moments, as we looked the other way with suppressed laughter.

For the main Chowk procession, we went to Papa's friend, Sri Amir Chand's house and stood in the ample verandah of the balcony, jutting out over the road where the procession came, which would be well past the midnight. By then half of us would be asleep. The rest barely kept awake,entertained themselves with idle chat and peanuts. Filmi songs were belted out from the loudspeakers. Poor Amir Chand would come from time to time to see that we all had enough stuff to eat specially the famous 'chat'.

Nowadays the ethos and spirit of Dussehra has disappeared. Youth are no longer interested in the age-old traditions. They are more attracted to the fast food and fast life. Simple pleasures of life are scoffed at, in favour of the internet and the social media.

At the Dussehra time, Durga puja was also simultaneously celebrated, by the sizeable Bengali population. Durga idols were tastefully put up in various 'mohalla pandals'. Incense and cymbals filled the air at the time of 'aarti'. On the last day of the celebration, the idols are immersed in the holy Yamuna and Ganga, with a promise to revive the Gods in the following year. Gods came back every year, in new hues and avatars. One must attune to the transient flow of life, and let the past be past.

Diwali is the most important and delightful festival in the calendar of the Hindus. It is the epitome of religious fervor, conviviality, and fun. The idols of Ganesh and Lakshmi, along with other gods and goddesses were tastefully decorated and put up as a jhanki in every house. Friends and relatives came to enjoy and appreciate the decoration and to offer their salutation to Goddess Lakshmi. We would, painstakingly, for weeks, collect the paper shreds called the 'tikkul' from ticker tapes of the PTI press, as well as sand, and colour them with vibrant colours, and lay them on the floor, as 'Rangoli'. I of course guided the whole ten day operation, roping in all my cousins and sisters to the unenviable task. On the day of Diwali, mother, taiji and chachiji narrated sacred tales to each other, and lighted the earthen lamps and candles with a special puja, as an offering and invocation to the Goddess Laxmi.

Now electric bulbs have replaced the earthen diyas.

We would put up the candles and earthen 'diyas', all over the house including the rooftop. Lakshmi puja was performed at about 8 PM, and ended with an aarti to the goddess, to invoke her blessings.

Now came the time for the main celebration. There would be a big firework show. Crackers were burst - bombs, anars, rockets, phuljharis, by all. Injuries happened once in a while, but they were a part of the game.

It was by then the time for food. Puries, kachories sweets and whatnots were laid out on the table, a grand culinary feat. All family members, lines of friends and relatives, would be welcome to participate.

In the end, after celebrating Diwali at our home, we went to our Nanaji's too, who would wait patiently for us. Earthen gods and goddesses were put on the floor, with colorful rangolis. Munni Mausi would do the chore. Each person offered the tika, roli, chawal, lawa, and flowers to Ganeshji and Lakshmiji. The earthen 'diyas' were lighted. Patakas, were burst as the finale.

Many times, we went to a late night film show as well, after the conclusion of all ceremonies. In the late night, everyone played the game of cards, called 'teen patia' with small stakes in a homely spirit. There would be at least ten to twelve people in the game. To lose on Diwali was considered auspicious.

One remembers **'raksha bandhan'** for the bondage between brothers and sisters. Both of my hands would fill upto the shoulders with rakhis from buas, sisters and cousins. Mother gave sweets and money to all sisters on my behalf.

There used to be a big fair at the Polo Ground, at the same time, near our house. It was a celebration for commemoration of martyrdom of some Muslim saints.

But for us it was fun time. It was called 'Gudia ka mela'. The chat, the tidbits, the sweets, the moving circus show and the merry go round engaged us breathlessly. Roasted bhuttas, new to the season and were the hot flavors of the day. Huge, decorated glittering 'tajias' were installed with a great fanfare, by the Muslim brothers at the mela area in honour of certain Muslim 'pirs'. The festival was an expression of mutual conviviality between the Hindus and the Muslims.

Festivals lead me to the experience of seasons in the plains of UP.

Seasons Changing seasons all the time bring disturbing and unsettling thoughts...

I had a strange fascination for the changing seasons of Nature. Seasons and especially the transition, the changing seasons, affected me. I got swept by emotions of yearning and longing, to catch and hold the passing season.

The world around us morphs. Colours, smells and sounds swirl through a daily and annual pattern. New patterns are put on display every season, which disappear and promise to return in new clothes the next season. The solar drum beats regularly to bring about the changes. The certainty is that we would again and again, witness the bounties and panorama of nature.

What does it mean to connect with seasons and with nature? It means becoming aware of the most important network around us and experiencing an enriching world around us. It means going to the roots of all that we have – health, work, life and culture – which are all subsets of nature. All living beings, plants, animals, humans are deeply connected and affected by the calendar of nature. In short it is Rousseau's 'Back to Nature' call to us.

As poet speculates on our very origin:

"Sunsets of fire bathed in azure.

Life formed from nothing as a spinner creates destiny from the chaos of sheared fibres.

We sit absorbed as the wind whispers 'Here you can find yourself!' rustling colours up through the petals."

Gulzar's evergreen song "Dil dhoondta hai phir wahi, phursat ke char din' from the film, Mausam', is so apt. The song is redolent with the images of different seasons of the year.

'Jaade ki narm dhoop ho, Aangan mein let kar...' Khushwant Singh wrote evocatively of the seasons. His piece on the advent monsoon in India, is incomparable. And Ruskin Bond, of course, has no peers as a worshipper of Nature, in the salubrious hills of Mussoorie.

Nature poets like Wordsworth, Byron, Shelley, Keats write hauntingly about the splendours of Mother Nature. American literature is chokeful of, nature worshippers like Poe, Emerson, Whitman, Dickinson, etc. Their powerful essays and sonnets are mind changing.

My childhood memories were ablaze with colours, of different flowers in different seasons of the year. I would plunge myself to imbibe the colours of spring, summer and winter and let their glorious, raucous, plumes burn the self.

Spring is the period of new feathery greenery, in every nook and corner of nature. Birds come back in abundance as the sun gets warmer. They start their bird songs at five in the morning, distracting the late risers no end in their sleep. Evergreens like mangoes are either laden with flowers which later become fruits or are clad in soft new pink leaves that mature later, if the tree decides not to flower that year.

Neem flowers profusely, the tree is covered with light green/whitish hazy blossom. It has a heady smell that attracts all, including the insects and bees.

The king of the flowering trees is the lime/lemon, with white blossoms and fragrance of deep citrusy note that transports one to a beauteous land of olfactory wonder. Citrus fragrance is the most popular of perfumes.

Rajnigandha blooms twice a year and whenever it does, all other fragrances pale into insignificance. The flame of the forest, palash, with its bright orange blossom, too waft the air. The frangipani oozes out its delicate heady fragrance, that makes one long for more. World famous perfumes are distilled out of the ethereal "Michaelia Camelia", which is one of the headiest fragrances, copied by Pierre Cardin. Thousand smells to choose from – an uphill task even for the world-famous perfumer, and collector, Luca Turin.

Perfumes are broadly of two types – natural, based on actual distilled essence of rose, jasmine, sandal, oud or lavender, and synthetic/molecular, concocted out of permutations of chemical molecules. The natural ones are expensive to procure, therefore the perfume industry relies more and more on artificially created fragrances. The most prized ones are 'prive collection,' the exclusive private collections of perfumers, for discerning customers, sold at skyrocket prices.

To sit in the night, under the canopy of stars in the garden, is like an invitation to Peter Pan to play his enchanted musical spell on nature.

As the sun hots more, in April/May, the bugle is sounded to the ears of the laburnum that it is time for it to throw out its yellow cascades. Glorious blooms of amaltas and gulmohar fill the roadsides with their blossoms. It is a riot of colours all the way - bright yellow and fiery orange. The rich fragrance rented the air. I would return from my school in the afternoon on the bike through the enchanted roads and passageways, lined with these trees. In addition, Jacarandas with their deep purple flowers dwarf all other colours into insignificance. Like Lucy of Wordsworth, I became a worshipper of nature.

The hills of Himachal, J&K, and the entire North East celebrated the season with hues of pinkish white flowers as apples, apricots, pears, rhododendrons and cherry trees started blooming. The whole vistas got alive with the rhapsody of flowers, for stretches and stretches of hills.

Peak **summer** sets in quickly and parched the land severely. The green grass turned brown and yellow. Not a blade of green was left. Birds forgot their songs, flowers wilted, and rivers dried up. The unrelenting loo would push the mercury to over 50 degrees. Animals and humans ran for respite.

At about this time, I used to enjoy watching the buildup of the strong summer wind amid the mighty neem and pipal trees in my house. There would be an initial lull. Then a strange humming sound would rent the air. An impending disaster, a foreboding! And audio warning would be followed by the visual beginning. To watch the storm shake the leaves of neem, pipal, gooler and other mighty trees reminded me of the 'Wild West Wind' of **Shelley**. In minutes, it would become a blackening dusty 'kali aandhi', billowing up whirls of dust and sand in the air. There would be a distant gurgling clap of thunder and darkness would descend.

Nature was heralding the advent of monsoon.

With the change of weather, air coolers installed in the houses would become redundant. The season of sleeping out in garden was also over. Sleeping out in summers was a norm in every family those days.

Expensive AC's were out of reach. Coolers were ineffective. Cool lawns with a sprinkle of water in the evening was the only option.

But there were drawbacks of sleeping out. Even the best of mosquito nets were not proof to the buzzing nocturnal creatures. They would attack in an army with their fangs and weapons, and an ominous war call. The horrid experience of the mosquito bites would be visible all over the swollen skin. There was no way out night after night.

The other drawback of sleeping out was that you had to time your sleep with the bird songs at the dawn. These winged creatures made such a racket from 4.30 am that it would be impossible to sleep longer. The strange thing was that their energies peaked in the mornings only. Thereafter they vanished, neither to be heard nor seen. But to be fair to these lovely creatures, their twitter and full-throated calls is a beautiful experience. Perhaps it is their mating call, perhaps it is an expression of joy at finding a worm, or perhaps it is a welcome cry for the new day.The flip side is that their sound had a therapeutic effect. Just to listen to the variety of music, belted out by them was an invitation to a peaceful, meditative start of the day. Binaural 'om' chants in the youtube, failed to evoke the same charm.

May/June is also the season of the king of fruits – the mango - of exquisite varieties, pedigrees and distinguished tastes – langar of Banaras, dashehri of lucknow, chausa, alphonso of Ratnagiri, to name a few, of an established royal lineage. And the melons (tarbooz), kharbuja and phalsa – summer is indeed the season of mellow fruitfulness as written by **John Keats.** The fruits ooze with sweetness and juice, in contrast to the surrounding dry air.

Rains

Mid-June announced the advent of cool breezes, thunderstorms and showers, after a testing period of waiting, and raising false hopes. But it came nevertheless. The advent of monsoon from the Arabian Sea was a sort of celebration in India. Mercury quickly plummeted from 45 to 35 degrees. The gathering clouds was a famed event, for the sight of which, people flocked to the Taj Hotel in Mumbai, directly hit by approaching dark ominous clouds from the Arabian Sea. Sips of the aromatic Darjeeling tea were the ultimate luxury.To feel the cool breeze of the monsoon, in every pore, and to treat the taste buds with the heavenly brew of the golden tips of the first flush – what a heaven!

One is lost in the web of nature's rhapsody. The raindrops beat softly on the window panes, like timorous wings of a bird. All is still. The stones, the gardens and the trees would be slowly crooned to sleep. The soft cadence of the pitter-patter of rain fades and dies, as one is lulled to drowsiness.

It was the time to savour the beauty of rain, the knocking on the windows, sometimes a gentle drizzle, sometimes a torrent. It was the time for wines and whiskies and parties.

The fields were filled with knee deep water. The schools are closed for the 'rainy day'. The Ganga swelled up in an ominous spate. 'Bade Hanumanji' would be completely submerged. Both Ganga and Yamuna became a virtual sea. The roasted 'bhuttas', the potato chops, and the samosas, with hot 'adrak' tea, from the 'khomchawallahs', on the banks of the river was a dream world.

Rains were followed by the short **winter** season, which again lasted for two to three months. Winters were severe, in the plains, and the mercury dipped to the sub-zero level, in many parts. This was the time to celebrate and rejuvenate. Flowers, of endless varieties, shapes, colours and smells filled the garden.

The enduring image of winter was the long morning walks we went on. It would be foggy and we would do five or six kms. We had buns and tea at the railway station. How utterly delicious they were! Butter would melt instantly in the mouth.

It was also the time for the red guavas of Allahabad.

Unique in look and taste, and grown best in the Khusro Bagh, the tomb of Nawab Khusro, surrounded by acres of land, the fruit was big, sweet and delicious. It tasted delectable with a pinch of black salt.

Allahabad city with its sights and sounds and flavors, its laid-back attitude to life, its festivals and seasons, lingers forever. All later events in life are judged in the scales, tipped in favour of Allahabad. The city has grown, new generation has come. Does the new generation value what we cherished? Has the age passed?

I lament the passage of things of the past, my childhood and my golden period of life. Do my friends and companions remember me? Doubtful! The pace of life, the time and age marches ahead. Past baggage is left on the wayside, as the mighty river of life rushes ahead.

My father's house has been sold now. I have stopped going to Allahabad. I miss the city. I feel desolate.

I feel uprooted. My city, my way of life, my memories have been disrupted.

Some old pictures of the family which show our humble beginnings

My Nanaji and Naniji

Joint family from father's side

Grandfather

My earliest memory of home was at 8, Hastings Road, opposite to the Allahabad High Court. It was a medium sized accommodation, rented from the Gandhis, owners of the Finaro Hotel, next door to us. We lived in a joint family with four uncles from the paternal side, with their formidably sized families. My grandfather was alive at that time and I have faint memories of him.

Grandfather, Sri Ganga Prasadji, breathed his last in his early seventies. The earliest memory I have of him, was of his daily trip to the Draupadi Ghat, on the banks of the Ganga, about five kilometres from the house. On one occasion, I too went with him. We walked on foot. Grandfather, Baba, was a devotee of Hanumanji. The small Ram Sita temple on the Ghat, was a peaceful quiet place, under a huge pipal tree. The panditji of the temple wore a Chandan tilak on his forehead. He would put the same tilak on us. The serene ambience of the place, awash with the fragrance of the agarbattis remains etched in my memory. From the verandah of the temple, I could see a faint shimmer of the Ganga River. The sand of the river brought down in flood, sprawled for miles. The alluvial sands were the best place for growing gourds like kharboojas, tarbooz and cucumbers, which grew best in the kachhar area. The fruits oozed with juice and sweetness. on his death bed, all seven uncles and buas crowded over Baba. He had been ill for some time. A photo of Hanumanji was swung over his blank eyes as his prana refused to leave him. He passed away in peace, over the lamenting family.

Grandmother

My grandmother, Dadi, was named Narayani, to us 'bahua'. She lived with us, at Nyaya marg, and later to the new house near the circuit house. We were regaled endlessly by her stupid talks and the harmless prattle, on many a lazy summer afternoons.

Jokingly, I once said to her 'Chhedilal' had come to meet her. Chhedilal was her 'sasur', father-in-law, of whom she was very fond. Due to memory lapses, she forgot he had died long back. She put on her ghunghat on reflex, as was the custom. To provoke her anger, I would ask innocently 'How is Chhedi? Or 'how is Khunni?, another character from her life. She immediately saw through my game and in anger she asked, 'Are you my Dada Pardada, calling them by name?' I would break into fits of laughter.

She always wanted her food in time. on one occasion it was delayed too much. When she saw 'khichri' come ultimately, she flew into rage and remarked, 'after so much noise and sound in the kitchen, I get only khichri. My cousin Guddi said eat it or I will take it away. She flared up and called Guddi a nagin. She disliked khichri. She was an old lady, nearing eighty, who in her advanced dotage, had only two desires in life - to eat and to sleep.

She heartily disliked her mother-in-law, who called her a 'bandariya' a she monkey. Indeed, on one occasion she had a painful encounter with a monkey, when she went upstairs to collect the dry clothes. She was bashed up by a big monkey. She would rejoice if we called her mother-in-law a black, ugly woman with big bulbous nose, and swollen eyes.

She suffered from occasional fits of epilepsy, due to which she could not be operated for her cataract. But we never stopped in our pranks and put an empty frame on her eyes without glass. She felt it were real glasses and was happy.

Her old lifelong wish seemed fulfilled. Immediatedly her vision also improved with the new spectacles. We also put nose ring, 'nath' on her and put a 'chunari' in her. Her happiness and coy smile we still treasure. It was great fun to sit and listen to her foolish talks. It used to be a hilarious comedy show.

She died one night, suddenly. I discovered her dead body early next morning in her bed, when I was leaving the house for BA examination. Some ants had crept into her body, which had turned cold and stiff by morning. I was frightened and called for mother. The last rites were performed on her on the next day.

She was such a darling! She never poked her nose into affairs of others. Once my mother came in the family after marriage, she withdrew herself from the family matters and mother took all responsibility. She kept herself to herself. She reminded me of the grumbling, comical Mrs. Brodie of Ayn Rand's

"Hatter's Castle'.

THE FAMILY

My Grandfather had five sons and three daughters, my uncles and buas. It is said that there were two more children who could not survive. Proof of fecundity of the grandparents!

The eldest son was Sri Bawan Das Agrawal, highly respected for his uprightness, who began his service in the subordinate judiciary. He was sent by the High Court for higher studies, to the Stanford University, California, from where, he completed his llm, in the first class, a rare achievement in those days. At the fag end of his career, he was elevated as a High Court judge in Allahabad. A man of simple and emotional nature, he showed brilliance and erudition in all his judgments.

He had seven children, all of whom were elder to me except the youngest one, Munna. They were my earliest companions and all my happy childhood memories revolved around them. What games and exploits were we not capable of! My childhood is strewn with the memories of those happy days. We went on long morning walks, we plucked mangoes from private houses and roadside trees, we played cricket, we played so innovative ball games, hide and seek, etc. We enjoyed the festivals, we staged home theatres. My childhood companions were Suresh Bhaiya, Dinu Bhaiya, Guddi, Rani, and Munna. My own sisters, Poonam and Abha were part of the group. Children of Bisun Chachaji, Anu, Pintu, Guria, all formed a motley group.

In summer holidays, cousins from Satna, Baby jiji, Raju bhaiya, Pipi, Kiku, Pappu, Tanu, Babloo came. From Faizabad Rita, lali, Guria, Udham Chand, Chhammo came.

From Gorakhpur Babli and Babloo, Minu came. Not to forget Chiku, Vandana, Archana and Gauri from Muzaffarnagar.

And Anupam, Tintu from Rae Bareli. A full house!!! A bedraggled group, dressed in simple clothes, ready for any game at any time. Firm reminders of the Dickensian age.

I became lonely when Tauji was transferred as a district judge to Saharanpur. I missed them. Only Munni jiji and Asha jiji remained in Allahabad to complete their postgraduation. They preferred my mother's company to that of their own mother.

The second son of my grandfather was Sri

Vishwanath Prasad Garg, who lived in Satna. He was tall, handsome and well built, a man of the world. He had a chequered adventurous career. In younger days, he worked ran errands in endless jobs in Calcutta. Later, he settled at Allahabad Bank, Satna, as the head cashier.

Satna was our real ancestral home, where the grandparents lived, but who later shifted to Allahabad,

Grandfather practiced law, in the kutchery. When he left for Allahabad, the house was occupied by my tauji, who lived with his seven children - three sons and four daughters. In summers we often went to Satna. There would be twenty people together in the house in the summer holidays. The chhat, the big roof, on the top floor, accommodated us all in the night. Beds were hired from a tent house.

There used to be an old dug well in the ground floor, which provided water when required. We would draw water from the well and loved to bathe with the buckets of cold water in hot summers. Clothes too were washed there. There was an iron 'jangla', frame, above the well, on the first floor. With our small feet, it used to be dangerous to walk on the jangla, without the fear of slipping through. But we revelled in the thrilling exercise.

Tauji was an accomplished yoga practitioner and much to our admiration, he would assume the upside down position of 'shirshasan' with aplomb and stay in the position for even an hour or so. While in the asana, he would command what to make for breakfast. No one dared to say a word to him. He was a terror in his own household. But he loved interacting with us, regaling us with incidents from his eventful life. Inevitably he brought buckets of juicy mangoes for all to gorge.

We went to see a movie, 'Jewel Thief', a Devanand Vyajantimala starrer. We reached late to the show and so special chairs were arranged for us in the balcony.

We also made short eventful trips to the Chachai fall, Chitrakoot and Govindgarh, famed for its white tigers.

Food was cooked in the old-fashioned mud chulha, with logs of wood for fire. It emitted lung crushing fumes. My Taiji, a gentle soul, spent the whole day at the chulha. She was very loving and considerate. She recounted funny tales about herself. Once while walking in the market, she tripped headlong into a bucket of water which she did not see. Much to her embarrassment, she climbed out of the bucket. We would explode with fits of laughter at her tales. She was mortally afraid of Tauji's outbursts.

A distant relative Bua, used to visit us sometimes. She pronounced 'sa' as 'sha'. We would deliberately ask about her visit to 'Shatna'. Prompt reply came 'Shatna mein badi barshat hui'. There would be loud squeals of laughter. She wondered what had happened. Later she realized that children were teasing her and making fun of her.

Father

The next in the family line was my father Sri Krishna Chandra Agrawal, the third child of my Grandfather, who was born in 1932, at Satna. Later he shifted to and started the legal practice in the Allahabad High Court. He had three offsprings, I was the eldest, and there were two younger sisters, Poonam and Abha. He had joined the chamber of Sri Shanti Bhushan as a junior lawyer. He had a fledgling practice, barely enough to keep the family together. But by dint of hard labour and his brilliant mind, he quickly rose up in esteem among the legal fraternity. Both the Bar and the Bench had the highest regard for him. He became the Chief Standing Counsel, and later the Advocate General of UP, at a very young age, arousing jealousy among his colleagues.

My mother belonged to the family of the then top publishers of Allahabad, Beni Prasadji. Her father was Sri Bishambhar Dayalji, who later became the Chief Justice of

Madhya Pradesh. He lived in a sprawling old house called

'Lal Bangla', at the Thornhill Road. My mother was a woman of many parts, a painter, an adept at Indian classical music, and a cook par excellence. She was a pious, gentle, peaceful and non-dominating soul, who understood her duties in the family.

She used to narrate the story of how she often went on a 'buggy' with Naniji to her grandparents at Katra, and thus cut her school on many occasions.

She was married to my father in an arranged manner. Father had just started his legal practice, but who later rose up to be the topmost lawyer of Allahabad. Further he was elevated from the Bar to the Bench in High Court of Allahabad. He later adorned top judicial posts as the Chief Justice of Rajasthan and then West Bengal High Courts.

Next in the line was Sri Vishnu Chandra Agrawal,

'Bishun', clerk in the High Court. He had four children.

Next were my two Buas, who were later married.

The eldest Bua, Ram Mani, was married to a well to do lawyer and lived in Faizabad. Their daughter, Sunita, Or Guria to us practiced in the Allahabad High Court, and who became a judge in the same court, is now elevated as Chief Justice of the Gujarat High Court. A rare achievement! An honor to all of us.

My middle bua, Shyam Mani, was responsible for dressing us up daily for school, as my mother was full time engaged in cooking for the family. She married Dr VK Gupta of Gorakhpur.

The youngest bua was Raj Rani, or Rajjo, who was very fun loving, sensitive and always wore a broad smile. She married Sri Santosh Kumar, an advocate, of a renowned, erstwhile zamindar family of Muzaffarnagar, with acres of orchards and real estate. In comparison, my buaji was very innocent and simple, who was in awe of her in-laws affluent people. She could never come into her own. She was happiest when she came to us in summers.

The youngest uncle was Ramesh Chacha, the beloved of all, who was not married at that time and who was a leader in all our childish games and exploits.

In sum, it was a motley collection, joined together with bonds of love and affection. All members lived in a crowded house with common bedrooms, living rooms, and toilets. The living hall would convert to a big bedroom, in the night, with cots laid out. The whole arrangement was dictated by the meagre income of the family – all members resigned to the pains and pleasures of an extended joint family.

That completed the cast from my father's side.

Maternal side

Nanaji Sri Bishambhar Dayalji, headed the family. A tall erect man, bespectacled with a distinguished look, with a religious aura. A man of principles, with little or no desires. He ws a devoted follower of Radha Swami Sangh and his mornings and evenings were occupied in worship of the reigning Guru of the sect. All family members were ardent followers of the sect and they joined him in satsang.

He was an advocate in Allahabad. He and Naniji would often come riding on a rickshaw to Papa and Mummy with fruits and sweets. His competence, dead honesty and uprightness led to his elevation as a High Court judge.He was transferred to MP High Court, Jabalpur. Thereafter he became the lok Ayukt of UP.

There were strange tales floating about the house he lived.

Nanaji lived in a huge house which had not been occupied by tenants for the thirty years, at the Thornhill Road. Queer stories circulated about it. It was haunted. At night if you went upstairs, footsteps followed you. There was a man in white pajamas, who walked close to you.

He sometimes even looked down from the skylight. Nanaji was able to get it at a very low rent. It was called al Bangla, or even Bhoot Bangla. The bungalow was huge with a verandah, five bedrooms, a huge drawing room and an office room, a courtyard and a kitchen and dining set, to boots. There was a big water tank for water needs. The bungalow was surrounded by half an acre of empty land, and a bricked boundary wall. There was a raised 'chabootra' in the open surrounding space for sitting. There was an ancient Pipal tree at the entrance. An old well near the tree was later filled up. In older times, there was a tomb here; actually it was a mazaar. The roof of the house was multi levelled. At the topmost level, was a baradari. Ghost stories emerged from here. At the fall of evenings, the roof got isolated. No one dared an encounter with a ghost.

I was bursting with curiosity. What if I just lurked for a minute? I went up surreptitiously, told no one. I went upto the baradari. Cautiously, looking back after every step, I climbed up. Nothing happened. Disappointed I started to climb down. Then I froze. I clearly heard footsteps following me. I turned back, there was nothing. I hastened my steps. Suddenly I saw a faint image in front – a man in white. It shimmered for a second under the weak bulb light. The shadow disappeared. I quickly ran down the steps, to the drawing room, with my heart racing high.

Was the shadow real or a hallucination? I still wonder.

Naniji was Laxmibai, belonging to the rich Katra family, that owned 'Laxmi Talkies', the cinema house. She suffered from periodical hysterical attacks for which Nanaji administered homeopathic medicines.

I had four mausis/aunts. Saroj Mausi, the eldest taught at Daulat Ram College, Delhi. A great academician, a music maestro in classical Hindustani and a great company. Sweet and soft spoken, she took us around in Delhi to a trip to all historical monuments.

She had no issues. Maybe Mausaji took her studies too seriously at the cost of other interests of life. I was the first born in my grandfather's family and she showered her love and blessings on me. Her pet name for me was Harsh. She knitted sweaters for me when I was a toddler. Mausaji passed away first and she led a lonely life at Agra at Hazoori Bhawan under the spiritual guidance of revered guru of Radha Swami Sangh, Sri Agam Prasadji, or Dadaji, after her retirement. His eldest brother, Kunwar ji Maharaj, who headed the Sangh then, had put the first drop of honey with a silver spoon. All of us were devout followers of the sect and made annual pilgrimage to Agra in summer. In fact the family of Dadaji were very close to Nanaji.

Asha Mausi was the fun lover, the firebrand of the family and she enjoyed life to the full. A resemblance **to Mala Sinha, the film actress,** was unmistakable in her face. Her love life became got into trouble and she was quickly married to Sri Narendra Garg, a scientist at CDRI, lucknow. She loved film music and purchased all HMV records. Her gramophone and collection of records was unenviable. Her other pursuit was photography. She was specially fond of me as a first child of the family. She would dress me up in costumes and flowers and take endless photographs. She bubbled with life. Her marriage was unhappy, although she had one offspring, Anuj. Somehow she lost her mental stability and would grow hysterical at small things. She was often taken to Noor Manzil, lucknow, for sedatives and electric shock. She was such a beautiful human - one cannot understand the ways of God.

My next Mausi was Daya, tall slim built, resembling **Nutan** in her simplicity. She was happily married to Sri Mangal Murti, a professor of Zoology at Balaghat. She was a very dignified person. Early death of her daughter, Reena, after delivery of a child, affected her deeply. She had two other sons Mayank and Chayank, both chartered accountants, and a daughter.

The youngest was Mridula, Munni Mausi, who now lives in Mumbai, and has a daughter, Mona and son, Manish, both happily married.

Mausiji was our constant companion, played with us, ate with us, climbed trees and slept with us. We went out for short walks to her College St Anthony's Convent and the Company Garden. We enjoyed badminton, in which she outplayed us with her superior height and reach. But I foxed her with my placements of the shuttle.

A swing used to be hung on the neem tree every monsoon by Mamaji. Five could sit on it together as it was a big plank of wood. My cousins Rani, Guddi and Munna would come with me. I pushed the swing so hard that poor Rani fell on the ground. I got a big scolding from Mummy.

My Mamaji, Sri Bhupeshwar Dayal was the only son in the family. He is a practicing lawyer at Allahabad High Courts. Fun moments and his frequent car trips and picnics are always remembered. He had twin hobbies of gardening and photography. He learnt guitar also. His beaming broad smile welcomed all with open arms.

My Nana's elder cousin came with his son and daughter in law, to live. Sri Visheshwar Dayal sported a small beard and was short stature. He had fixed a reading light over his bed. From all appearances, he had probably pinched it from a railway coach. We would fiddle with it and ask him deliberately where he got it from. Furious, he would shout and drive us out from his room. When Nanaji came to know about it, he asked him to remove it.

His son was called Baby, my Mamaji, although he was a big fat hulk. He ran a small homeopathic clinic, hardly able to make both his ends meet. His wife, Mamiji, was sweet, amiable and perfect company to everyone. They had no issues, however much they tried, which was their consuming sorrow of life. later they shifted to a house of their own.

This completes the **Dramatis Personae, from both, father's and mother's side.**

Memories of the joint family….

In our joint family at Allahabad, there were a dozen cousins of almost all ages. In holidays, more would join from Satna, Faizabad, Gorakhpur and

Muzaffarnagar. Full house meant 41 members.

Marriages naturally were a crowded affair. If you add the extended family, it would be no less than hundred members from the home front alone. Days and nights came and went. Everything happened mechanically. There were no hotels those days. So we would live together and have a grand family party on a daily basis for the period of the marriage. The jokes, the leg pulling, the repartees and the sheer constant pressure of a thronging crowd kept us engaged. It was a perennial party. Twenty six of us took a ride on the rickety old Landmaster on one occasion. The car was shaken but we were not stirred.

Cooking was a daily ordeal in the kitchen. To prepare four meals a day for twenty-five people was not a joke. My mother, taijis, chachiji accomplished the daily feat. Those were the days when there was no cooking gas. Traditional mud chulha with logs of wood and coal was used. The fumes were intense and choked our eyes and lungs. My poor taiji at Satna suffered and died of TB after prolonged use.

Summer holidays were pure fun. In the pock-marked garden, with hardly a blade of grass to boast, we had our daily games and activities. It was indeed an apology of a garden with a few patches of grass, that had escaped our attention. The onslaught of the ball games did not spare a single plant. Poor, sturdy guava and lemon trees withstood the daily attack gamely.

Cricket was the favourite game, with the tree bark or a wall serving as the wicket. Only a bat and a ball were required. I was the natural leader. Another popular game was 'seven tiles' and then , a roughergame, 'gend tadi', where you hit the other players as hard as posible. No apologies were required. It soon degenerated into a game of attrition.

There would be a severe reprisal later.

My father, worked in the home office. Naturally our full-throated shouts and yells of joy during the melee disturbed him. I was the villain of the piece and often got slapped. The dignity of my leadership was tattered in seconds. Poor frightened cousins and playmates immediately made themselves scarce and escaped the wrath. I usually bore the brunt. But father's temper cooled down quickly. We were back to our games in no time, continuing now, a little more sedately.

I once remembered that at about 9 in the night, some full-throated shouts and shrieks disturbed my father and he came out of his office in temper. In panic, I hid myself in the mogra bushes. My father looked around for me. He asked everyone but no one knew where I was. Everyone had pity for me. Fear was palpable. I hid among the dark bushes for more than an hour. Dinner time had come and still there was no trace of me. My uncles, cousins searched everywhere. I remained in my hiding ground. Searching, Bishun Chacha came close to my hideout, but could not see me in the dark. By now everyone was worried and panicked at my disappearance. Even father got anxious. Where had the six-year-old kid disappeared? Search parties were sent to nearby areas and markets. I just remained hid. I started thinking I'll get up early morning and collect all the mogra flowers. I started enjoying the smell of mogra flowers in my hideout. But how long could I stick? I finally decided to come out. Defeated but not vanquished! I awaited another bout of outburst from my father. But the storm had subsided. I quietly joined others. There were happy shouts of joy and relief from all. Relief prevented them from asking me more questions.

Even father was felt relieved in the heart.

Papa was an amiable and amicable man, with a lot of charm in his personality. He was humble to the core and his interpersonal relationship was impeccable. It came to him naturally. He was either working in the

High Court, lower court or in his home chamber.

Clients kept him busy 24/7 which he seemed to take in in his stride and enjoyed the daily chore. His practice picked up. He joined the chamber of the senior lawyer, Mr. Shanti Bhushan. A paltry two and a half rupees, was earned by him on the day of my birth, 2/6/1956.

Born and bred in Satna, he shifted to Allahabad for practice. He rented an old house in Badshahi Mandi, where I was born. By the dint of hard work, his career rise was spectacular.

When I was three years, he shifted to the new rented house, at Hastings Road, conveniently opposite the High Court. Not exactly penurious, but he had seen hard days. The burden of the jumbo joint family must have weighed upon him. But he was always cheerful and lived from moment to moment, spreading joy and laughter.

We children i.e. I and my two sisters never got the benefit of his company or counsel. A pin drop silence would befall the house at his approaching footfall from the High Court. We, cousins et al, would quickly hide behind the books. This satisfied him and after tea, he settled down to his office work, and he no longer troubled us through the evening.

My annual report card of the school was shown to him through mother. Since I always topped, he had nothing to complain. Neither a word of encouragement nor praise came from him. Just a satisfied grunt. He had psychologically distanced himself from his own children.

My interests and hobbies

I had a fascination for plants and flowers.

I remember I used to watch with awe as seeds of dhania, radish and methi would sprout from the soil IN THE crisp winter air. The topsoil was left loose. Little feeble heads would emerge, breaking the hard crust. The seed pods would emerge upturned, seed up, from the soil, and later would convert to the first leaves of the new plant. I would watch the little magic every morning in my garden and wonder at the sheer wizardry of Nature. After the first shoots, the plant would add leaves rapidly. Some inner force drives the mechanism. Secrets of life hide in small things.

My childhood fright

There was an incident which frightened me no end that time.

There was an old man, called Shikari, who lived in a row of outhouses, near our house. He was invariably followed by two or three dogs when he went for a walk. We kept our distance from him. He was tall, in his fifties, with a gaunt gait. He wore thick glasses. He always carried a lathi and a shoulder bag. He would sit on his cot after his walks.

On one occasion I happened to stand close to him, with others. He had rested his lathi on the cot. Suddenly he flashed his teeth and gave a sinister smile. His teeth gleamed in the fading evening light. I was frightened and I ran. There was something scary about him. I told my mother he wanted to kidnap and eat me. Mother looked at me sympathetically and went on with her work.

On another occasion I chanced to see him again. My cousin Munna was with me. Again, he flashed his teeth, moving them up and down in his mouth. We ran away in fright. We were told that he was a shikari, a hunter, who hunted for small children and kept them in his bag to eat them later. A story was that he was a dog eater too.

The third time I met him was with other street boys. I stood at a safe distance, my heart in my mouth in anticipation. Again the old man looked up and moved his gleaming white teeth menacingly at me. He uttered a guttural, gurgling sound. In sheer terror I ran from the macabre man at top speed. He pointed his finger at me all the time.

It later transpired that he wore an ill fitting denture which he moved up and down in an effort to adjust them.

Mangoes brought me a great sense of joy. The first thing in the April month I did was to get up early and go on a hunt for raw mangoes, There were lines of mango trees at the Polo Ground. I with Rani, Guddi, Munna and Poonam went on the morning stroll along the mango vistas. We were rewarded with the fruit for our effort in daily jaunts. April end/ May was the time when schools closed. There used to be a competition among us to collect the most number of mangoes. We used to be so mad that we would begin our morning prowl at 5.30 in the morning, as the early bird caught the worms. Mangoes grew bigger in size as days went by. We were happy to hand over our little treasures to Mummy, who would make 'chatni' and 'panna' out of them.

Once I recall during our morning walk, we noticed the biggest, luscious fruits in Allahabad Bank building. I dared to cross the boundary and jump inside. In a trice the chowkidar pounced on me. He had been wondering who had been stealing the mangoes. I was frightened as he pulled me and threatened to report to the manager and to father. My companions disappeared and I was left alone to face the music. After some altercation, the chowkidar let me go. I returned home sheepishly down faced. But our mango trips continued, so irresistible was the lure of the fruit.

I had two other companions who aided me in my mango hunt - the little son and daughter of our domestic help. They would give me big 'kalmi' mangoes from Justice Satish Chandra's garden. I proudly flaunted them as my trophies.

The romance of mangoes has not died yet. Whenever I see a tree laden with mangoes, my childhood memories are revived. How I wish to again pluck the fruits from the burdened tree!

There was once a mango party at my Papa's friend, Ram Manoharji. I was introduced to all luscious varieties – 'langra', chausa, dashahari, badaam, totapari, alphonso, the sucked ones, etc. It goes without saying that after gorging them all, I had a very upset stomach.

Swimming in the Ganga

When I was in the intermediate class, XII of UP Board, I was eaten by the bug to learn swimming. So in the summer vacation, in the mornings, I used to go on a cycle with my cousin Deepak, to the Rasoolabad Ghat of the Ganga, about ten kilometers from the house. Some parts of the river were deep and the current was treacherous. My hairs rise up still when I remember an incident which almost drowned me. While swimming one day, I was caught in a powerful cross current. I lost the purchase of my feet on the river bed completely and was carried helplessly by the powerful flow of the Ganga. Panic had struck. And I had nowhere to look for help. By providence, a small fisherman boat came and with effort, I was somehow able to climb on it and saved my life by the skin of my teeth. I did not tell anyone about the incident. But that was the end of my swimming trips to the Ganga. I learnt the hard way that one cannot flirt with the mighty Ganga without the attendant peril. I joined a pool in the city at the 'Yatrik' hotel and learnt swimming and thus fulfilled my passion.

We used to go frequently in fact weekly, to grandfather's (Nanaji) place, at the Thornhill Road. It was said the 'lal bangla' was reputed to be haunted. It was reported that white shadows followed you on the roof, in the night. Nanaji was a devout follower of 'Radhasoami', and the divine force of his worship/bhajans, mornings and evenings, drove the ghosts out. We never saw them prowling ever, although I secretly wished I did encounter one or two.

My play companion was Munni Mausi, only three years older, was full of spirit and joy for life. So many times, with my two smaller sisters, Poonam and Abha, we enjoyed

Munni Mausi's delightful company and her innovative stories and games. She was skilled in sewing, knitting, cooking, and all activities that engaged us with fun. Her marriage took her to Rae Bareli/Bhilai. Mausaji was genial, courteous and respectful. But somehow their marriage soured and they separated. Without her the house was empty.

Buaji

I was also fond of my youngest Buaji, Rajjo, who got married to Santoshji, a lawyer in Muzaffarnagar. Santosh Phuphaji was a rich landlord by birth, a zamindar of Muzaffarnagar. Even after marriage Buaji loved to come to Allahabad. She was closely attached to Mummy. All of us spent such hilarious time together, be it market, or coffee house or cinema. She was not averse to seeing two or three movies in a day, back to back.

I remember our joint trip to Darjeeling, Gangtok and Bhutan. My mother and Buaji were both a little overweight, and my Phuphaji would enjoy the sight of their puffing and huffing, as they trudged to the rest house, in their rolly polly climb upto the hill. In a good natured way, he called them footballs, much to their umbrage.

We were introduced to the Chinese/Western cuisine for the first time at the Gangtok State Guest House.

We were all in a little awe at the lush carpeted rooms, the food and the courteous services of the English House keeper. Buaji's youngest daughter then, Archana, did not know what to do with the food served or the cutlery laid out. She was an embarrassed child of six years then. She contented herself with just tomato sauce.

I used to be an avid storyteller. Children would collect around me in the night time in the beds, under the stars, on the roof. It used to be magical, as the stars filled the sky one by one. We had identified them from star charts. I would ask them which star you would like to go after death? The answer used to be Pole star, or orion or Ursa Major, the constellations I had identified for them. There used to be so much excitement.

In a low voice I would regale them with tales, some read and some imaginary. Archana would lap them up with wonder, all my weird and grotescue tales. I loved to recite the scary ones, involving ghosts and haunted houses. Bram Stoker's Dracula captured the imagination of everyone. Buaji, cousins, Chachiji all cocked their ears one by one as Dracula advanced his evil progress. We would go downstairs, so as not to disturb the parents.

The tale of the Count Dracula horrifies and and his blood sucking rituals still sends shivers. My voice assumed more and more sinister tone as the story advanced. There would be pin drop silence poor Meena got victimized. As the long story continued, hour after hour, other members too joined. In the end, my little sister would ask does the Dracula still live? I would say, yes the Dracula still lives. In fright, she would ask is it still alive? With relish, I would say it comes out even at present time from the toilet seat. My sisters and Buaji did not go to toilet for the next two days.

On one occasion, we went to Mussoorie, an annual feature for us. Daya Mausiji, Mausaji, Mamaji, Munni Mausi and my family Papa, Mummy, Poonam, Abha and me, all made a little party. We took a lodge for night stay, in the market area. We all went to buy utensils and groceries for dinner. 'Tahari' was prepared and we all quietened the rats in our stomach. Next was the story telling time. Mausaji was a florid person and he quickly told the horrid stories of ghosts and demons. 'Bees Saal Baad' was fresh in our minds. Mausaji and Mamaji, with their folded knuckles took the daylight out of our young minds, as they enacted the 'panja,' in the mist and fog of Mussoorie, which had entered our room through the open window.

Mussoorie was replete with the tales of the Savoy Ghost of Savoy Hotel, and the Spirits of the Camel Back Road, where an English couple had met with an accidental death, whey fell from a horse fall.

Sisters

Being the first born, mummy had great affection for me. My sibling sisters were younger by three or four years.

Poonam, the elder one, was a carefree, happy person, never overly worried, with a ready loud laughter. She did M.Sc. in Botany from Allahabad. She never bothered anyone about her studies. She had some friends who kept her engaged.

The younger one, Abha, was of a more sensitive nature, who would get worked up on small issues. She had English Literature in B.A. But somehow, examinations put her in jitters. I had to drill the curriculum, the English plays and poetry into her mind repeatedly to make her understand. She would try to learn her lessons by heart. It looked like it was Mummy's and my exam, rather than hers. But in the end, she did well in B.A.

Both are married now. Poonam has settled in Brisbane, Australia. She has held jobs in management/finance in different companies. Her husband Anurag took a courageous decision at the beginning of his career, and chucked his job in the NTPC to move to the Down Under. He had no regrets later. Poonam has a job in IT and financial areas.

Abha is married to Harish who has now retired as an

Additional Member in the Central Railway Board,

Delhi.

I was always close to them in the heart but never expressed it.

My father's new house

My father built a house of his own at some distance from the old one, near the Circuit House, a posh area of the city, in 1971. But my childhood memories were connected more with the earlier house. The exploits we indulged into in the mango season, the climb on the guava tree in the garden, where I had found a hidden perch, the joy of just doing nothing - what a storehouse of happiness it was!

The new house, near the circuit house saw us complete our education. The marriage of so many of our family – my four cousins, daughters of the eldest tauji, BD Agarwal, and my next Tauji, Sri Vishwanath Garg, my youngest Chachaji Ramesh, and of course me and my two sisters were solemnized here. In every way it was a lucky and auspicious house.

My parents were unique in many ways. Papa was so sensitive he could not see any one cry. Tears gushed to him also. He wished to see all of us happy. He brought gifts for everyone, all uncles, buas and cousins, when he came back from his trips from Bombay or Delhi. His large heartedness endeared him to all his friends and visitors. He was blessed with a big heart. He got a meteoric rise in his career, at which everyone rejoiced. While the eldest Tauji was a district judge, Papa got elevated to the Bench at a very early age of 47 years. My Tauji was very happy for him. However this did spew some jealousy among his colleagues at the Bar.

School Days

The first school I went to was a kindergarten, 'Little Folks Nursery', at Allahabad, which had about 1000 odd children. I remember I dreaded to go to the school. There was an Anglo Indian singing teacher, who used to take daily singing lessons with us. While some children were good and joined heartily in the group songs, I could never come to terms with the English hymns and songs. I would try to fake the lip movement, extremely tormented by the proceedings.

The plump old teacher, Mrs Gentle, would eye me with a glassy glint as she could make out my false lip movements. I was singled out on more than one occasion for punishment. I was never able to learn singing.

The school was upto Class I only after KG, so I continued there even after KG. Officially it was a kindergarten only. When I went for admission to the next school, I was made to repeat Class I, as the new school did not recognize Class 1 of the earlier school. The new school was a co-education school, called 'Girls High School'. My two younger sisters also studied there.

I studied upto Class III there. Thereafter I was shifted to 'St. Josephs' College', the best known school in Allahabad, run by a Catholic establishment, with a Cathedral and a Chapel, as marks of the Christian institutional presence. I studied from Class IV to ISCE, which replaced the earlier ISC.

What memories of the period do I carry?

I remember the long lunch hours when all children brought out their lunch boxes in the play field under the trees. Quite a few were sent hot lunch from their homes. There used to be flocks of hungry eagles, who would, at the sight and smell of food, swirl around, flying menacingly in circles above us. Unsuspecting children were attacked, their sandwiches and parathas snatched by the eagles' sharp talons. The birds dived accurately from nowhere. I would watch these powerful birds with fascination, listen to their shrill cries, if they managed to snatch the food. I was particularly fascinated by their trajectory of flight, the way they soared up and turned back at a 360 degrees swoop, in their majestic manner. One moment they soared away from you, the next moment they traversed menacingly back in your direction, in a split second. I was left in a daze by their sweeps and swirls. What magnificent creatures they were, now no longer sighted easily.

Our headmaster was Father Rego, short in height, stockily built, bespectacled with very thick lenses and a short goatee beard. He was nicknamed 'billy goat' by the students. He wore a Roman catholic white cowl of a priest, but he looked more like a Jesuit priest. Very well read, he took English Language classes with us. For help of the students, he had written books on proverbs, idioms, essay writing, etc. The books were, of course made compulsory. All proverbs and idioms were meant to be learnt by heart. He was at one time, reputed to have failed the entire Class X in English and did not give promotion. The students, rich, poor, or elite background, were very upset. In our class too, he showed no kindness. To get 40 out of 100, the pass mark, was an achievement. I secured 44 and was at the top of the world. He made us learn the hard way. He was very supple with his cane as well, and he chose the bony parts of the hand for treatment. In short, he was a terror.

Once while he moved up and down the class, one naughty boy poked out his fountain pen into his cowl, and blotted it with ink. Next day, he caught the boy in the act and muttered, 'Now I know how I spoil my clothes'. The boy was suitably caned.

As I reached the higher classes, I was especially fascinated by Geography, the study of different lands and people. History was a bore. I also liked nature studies and Biology. I was good at science subjects like Chemistry, Physics and Additional Mathematics. Some teachers at St Joseph's were par excellence. I remember Mr. Carlyle D'cruze for Chemistry, Mr. Francis Moore for being an excellent class teacher in Class VI, Mrs Guha for Shakespeare's 'Macbeth', Mrs Mehta for Bernard Shaw's 'Pygmalion', Mr DC Pande for Additional Mathematics, and of course Father Rego, the headmaster, for English Language. His English, both written and spoken, was impeccable. His comportment and demeanour, and his ever obliging cane in hand, filled us with respect and terror.

College days

After doing ISC from St Joseph's College, Allahabad, I switched to Political Science, Economics and English Literature in BA, with a mind to graduate in law, later, and practice in the Allahabad High court, like my father. But things turned out differently.

I was selected for NSTS scholarship, which meant I would be required to pursue my studies in the science stream after the XII standard. This was essential if I wanted to continue getting scholarship, which was about Rs.1500 per month. I was also offered M.Sc. at Pillani (BITS) on the strength of selection in NSTS. At about the same time I was selected in IIT Kharagpur in Mechanical Engineering. But I was to join

Humanities for further studies.

I was always a lonely child, enjoying in my own way, never in much need of a company. I was not even overly ambitious or coveted for any particular kind of a career. If I did well in class, it was my natural flair. I was consciously and uncomfortably shy of public speaking. I did not know what to say to others, and kept myself to myself. Some complex I developed early in life! But I was just content with my affairs. I could not mix with other friends. So I did not have people to confide my secrets and ambitions. My only friends were the classmates at school. They all got selected for IITs. I was selected in NSTS, and by the virtue of this selection, I got an offer from BITS, Pillani for postgraduation. later I qualified for Metallurgical Engineering at IIT Kharagpur. But I preferred and joined Arts/Humanities at the Allahabad University.

University days…

I chucked it all and after Intermediate, joined B.A. in 1977, at the Allahabad University. Subjects chosen were Economics, Political Science and English Literature. All of them were close to my heart. And with these non-scoring subjects, I secured the second position in the merit list. I also got medals in Economics and Political Science.

In English Literature, my favourite and the star attraction of the Department was Sri Manas Mukul Das. His cool, calm and smiling face gave him the epithet of the smiling Buddha. Indeed his demeanour typically resembled Swami Vivekananda. His rendering of 'Break, break, break,' of Tennyson was soul stirring. The English Romantic poets were his forte and the insight he gave into the subtle nuances of verses of these poets was unsurpassed. The magic of his teaching would cast a lasting spell on us. We all became a Keats or a Shelley in those days.

Alok Rai, the grandson of Mahatma Gandhi, took English Drama classes with us. Sri Arvind Krishna Mehrotra, the well known poet also belonged to the English Department Faculty.

My favourite teacher in Economics was Prof. DK Ghosh whose explanations and clarifications of the complicated concepts of micro and macroeconomics were brilliant.

In Political Science, the stalwart was Prof Amba Dutt Pant, who was revered by students. He would spend the entire year teaching Plato and Aristotle, without touching other Greek philosophers, in the course.

I joined MA, in Political Science in 1979, where I secured the second position in the merit list, by the virtue of which I was given ad hoc lectureship in the University. After teaching for a year I was selected in the IAS in MP cadre in 1982.

During my university days I had picked up writing skill and I contributed occasional articles to the local daily, Northern India Patrika.

I did LL.B. after MA. In the heart of hearts, I wished to quietly practice in the Allahabad High Court, like my father, who had worked hard to rise as a top lawyer, with a roaring practice. He was later elevated to the High Court Bench at Allahabad. He became the Chief Justice of Rajasthan and later, of West Bengal. Due to internal politics, he missed elevation to the Supreme Court of India. My paternal grandfather Sri Ganga Prasad, too, was a lawyer, a deeply pious man. My maternal grandfather Sri Bishambhar Dayal, was the much respected Chief Justice of the High

Court at Madhya Pradesh, again almost a saint figure, and highly venerated in the legal circles. But life had other dimensions in store for me. I joined the IAS.

I had a few friends Sunil Gupta, who lied with his father, who had a roaring practice at the High Court, and owned a big house. It was clear from the beginning that Sunil would join his father in practice which he did.

There was Rohit N andan, son of Justice Yashoda Nandan, who got into IAS with me.

There was Sharad /v armawho was closest to me. "He was a very nervous person by nature. Examination fear would make him a jelly fish. Unfortunately he died early in his forties, which devastated his parents and wife.

Sunil married Priyamvada, but Rohits marriage went on the rocks. Since then he has been living with hie mother and he is happy.

My cousin sister became very devoted to me at that stage. She lived in Satna and she came to Allahabad in summer holidays every year. In the heart of hearts we liked each other. Now both of us are separately married with no regret. She is still very sweet.

I maintain a reasonable physical figure, and I work hard at the gym. I suffered from a slipped disc at the gym which slowed my pace of life. I recovered from it slowly.

Marriage

I was married in 1983, to Nishi. Her father was Sri NK Shinghal, (IPS), then the DG of Police in places like Delhi, Chandigarh and Mizoram. Marriage was performed in Chandigarh. My father in law was close to Rajiv Gandhi, at Mizoram.

My house in Allahabad was crammed with relatives and guests. Every day was a celebration of sort. Nishi was a dignified, graceful person, with a lot of quiet intelligence, who was a little confused in the beginning, in the midst of so many people. I was too shy to talk or confide in her much. We went to Kathmandu, Nepal, on our first visit together. We stayed at Soaltee's Hotel, which had the only Casino at that time. Pashupati Nath temple used to be crowded and full of aggressive monkeys. And it was very dirty also. We spent three days in Kathmandu.

Thereafter Nishi had to stay with family for sometime. I was posted in Rewa as Assistant Collector and got very poor, government accommodation. The heat and dust of Rewa was gruesome to say the least. I was posted in difficult areas like Barwani, Alirajpur, Dharamjaigarh, etc, one after the other, in the span of first three years of service. I then became Collector at Sidhi. I was then posted to Damoh and later, to Surguja, as Collector, These were short tenures, lasting from one to one and a half years each. I got a chance for a settled life only after being posted at Bhopal.

My son

My son was born in Nineteen ninety two, at Delhi. I stayed with my in-laws at that time. His face was as peaceful as the Buddha. I was blessed with a beautiful child. When he was not asleep, he gave a big smile if he happened to catch the eye. He would throw up his limbs in glee. He would go to all rooms in the house, end to end, on his small legs, as a toddler. He would be triumphantly happy if he happened to stand up on his own, with no support.

As he grew up, he became a naughty child, who had a mind of his own. one can say even precocious in earlier days. He loved cricket and easily beat me with both bat and ball at our old residence in Bhopal. But in 'carrom board' I got the better of him. He would quickly lose interest in the game, after losing.

He had a keen eye and fascination for the mobile phone and the computer, which were toys to him. He had great love for mangoes and he would gorge them down in a trice. He felt close to Mummy and Buas and their children and interacting with them. He was happy in the company of Nana and Raghu, my sisters children. Mummy brought samosa and jalebi for him every day in the morning breakfast. He turned out to be a foodie, loving the good things of life.

His first kindergarten school was 'love Dale.' After kindergarten, he went to The Campion School Bhopal, where he completed his schooling. He then went to BITS, Pillani for Mechanical Engineering and thereafter, he was selected for the University of Illinois, Urbana Champaigne for ME and then Ph.D.in the same field. He has won accolades from his fellow colleagues and the scientific community. A few of his scientific papers have been published in major journals. He completed the Ph.D. in September 2020. He has decided to join academics and he continues with his research fellowship in the Berkeley University. He is betrothed to his fiancée, Lucille, of the French/American origin.

Career – New beginnings

I was selected in the IAS in 1982 and joined service in September 1982. I remember the day I departed for Mussoorie. Almost all friends and family had come to the railway station to see me off, some with a smile and some with tears. All with a heavy heart. I was forlorn, miserable. I knew that my father would have a difficult time with his colleagues, who were usually self-seeking. He trusted people easily to his own detriment. He allowed people in his bedroom without hesitation.

People took advantage of association with him. Stern eye from Mummy and disapproval from me kept him in check. His gushing nature often put him in difficulty.

The consolation was that Santosh Phuphaji and Chikoo, my cousin, from Muzaffarnagar, accompanied me to the Lal Bahadur Shastri National Academy of Administration.

It was a parting of ways – the start of a new life.

Somehow, at the time, I was not comfortable, and felt unsettled. I would have loved to live with my 'Climson Glories' and 'Queen Elizabeths' at Allahabad. What a beautiful and well stocked nursery was maintained at the Alfred Park!

The LBS Academy at Mussoorie was beautiful, life was pleasant and anonymous, meaning you were one in the crowd of similar officers and it was upto you what you wanted to do with your time.

Food was consistently bad, day in day out. Our group detested the kachchi roti and insipid dal served.

Invariably we went out to Harry's, or to the Mall.

I loved the walks in the town upto the library point, further down to Landour. Food used to be on the top of our agenda in our jaunts to the market. The chat of Kulri Bazaar reminded me of Allahabad.

I frequently strolled to the Company Garden behind the Academy. I loved my perch, a high bench near the Glass House, in the Garden, a haven for nature lovers, surrounded by the giant sized begonias, dahlias and roses. From my vantage point, the vistas were breathtaking – the descending valleys of Dehradun on one side, and the ascending mountain peaks of Badrinath, Bandarpoonch, etc, on the other, – all enveloped in a blue haze.

On clear winter days, one realized that the whole area, including the Academy itself was engulfed with snow. There would be snow clad mountains end to end. A thick haze of clouds completely blocked them on most days.

Rooms in the Happy Valley Hostel were double seated, my partner was a Bengali guy of some other service, who loved to play Rabindra and Nurul Hasan sangeet in the morning.

The impression that I still vividly carry of the Academy is that of the superb library, the earlier one. It was glazed with glass panels all around and commanded a lofty view of the sheer blue valleys straight below. The book collection was superb, and one realizes the number of painstaking years and money it must have taken to put them together. My vistas of knowledge increased at an accelerated pace. In the cool, crisp air of the mountains, I was indeed lost in the world of books. Later when we returned back to the Academy after the district stint, the library was completely burned down. Rumours were rife that it was not an accident, but a deliberate work. What an irreparable loss!

We went for 'Bharat Darshan' tour, from the Academy.We covered Maharashtra, Tamil Nadu, Andhra Pradesh, Kerala, etc

An old picture with companions of 1-82 batch.

At the end of the Foundation Course, I won medals in Political Science and a recognition for Yoga Demonstration.

Early Postings

My professional life began from IAS Academy....

After completing the Foundation Course at Mussoorie, I received my first posting order for Assistant Collector, Rewa. There was a lot of excitement among us at Mussoorie. This was the first field posting, after completion of the First Phase at Mussoorie. After completing a year at the district assigned, we were supposed to join again at LBSNAA, for the Second Phase of the training of one month.

Rewa was close to Allahabad, my home. It was a dull and drab district, only about 125 kms from Allahabad. I remember the first day I joined there. I landed there by bus, with a small luggage. An old rickety jeep had come at the bus stand with a tehsildar to receive me. I was taken to the Commissioner's office straightaway. The Commissioner was Mr Arun Kumar, indeed a very genial person. The quarter allotted to the AC was a small two room house. The AC's house was behind the Collector's. In the beginning I was alone, and a poor peon used to cook for me. Mr. Sumit Bose was the Collector, a 1976 batch officer, and a gem of a person, with no airs at all about him. A favourite dish for him was 'ande ki bhurji' at that time, which I shared a number of times with him.

I was married while in Rewa. After marriage, I and Nishi frequently went to Mr. Sumit Bose, and his wife, Chandra, for company and to get back to touch with the reality we were used to, in a desert of indifferent land and people. Mrs. Bose would make it a point to invite us to lunches and dinners in her house. We were hopelessly unsettled and disorganized, as far as the kitchen was concerned, at that time in the new house.

There was nothing much to write home about in the district. I used to sit with Mr Bose in his office and observe him dealing with the endless queue of petitioners and the public. I was sent to the block, Teonthar, for block development training, for a week. Other trainings were scheduled at departments like mining, excise, irrigation, MPEB, PWD, Revenue, Police, etc, as per the diary prescribed by the LBSNAA. My reports and experiences had to be signed by the Collector before submission to the Course Director, Sri Alok Sinha at LBSNAA in the second phase of training.

The overriding emotion I had in Rewa was that of uprooting from my home at Allahabad. Fortunately it was only 125 kilometres by bus. I would go to Allahabad at the weekend and come back on Monday morning. Sometimes, I was pulled up by the Collector, but I think he understood the psyche of a probationer. The closeness of Allahabad was a contributing factor. I remember that a review meeting of agricultural production, revenue and law and order matters of Rewa division was taken by the then Chief Secretary of the state, Sri Brahma Swarup at Khajuraho. The meeting was considered as a terror exercise by all collectors of the division. CS was very tough and would get down to the bottom of the issues. As an AC I would amusedly observe the discomfiture of the collectors, as they interacted with the CS.

Rewa was the famed home of white tigers, which were kept at a sanctuary in Govindgarh. This natural Albino strain looked stately and majestic. People from all over the country flocked to have a peep at them. Now of course the Albinos have multiplied by breeding and they can be found in many locations in the world.

I remember the visit of the Prime Minister Mrs Indira Gandhi to Satna, where Sri. DS Mathur was the Collector. I went as AC Rewa, to observe at the first hand, how arrangements were made for a VVIP visit. My batch mate Raghav Chandra was at that time AC Satna. There used to be unending drills with the police guys and the district administration. The Circuit House was totally revamped. Details like who would serve the juice and what kind, were meticulously discussed. It was an instructive learning.

Postings....

My first regular posting as SDM/SDO was on other the end of the sprawling state, on the western end, bordering Maharashtra, at Barwani, after the completion of the second phase of training at Mussoorie. The residence of the SDO at Barwani, was an old royal house, called 'Mor Bangla', boasting of 24 rooms. Of course most of the rooms were unliveable holes, leading from one into the other. There were beautiful statues of Lord Adinath at Bawan Gaja, the tallest in the country.

My stint in Barwani was short. On the very first day of my posting in Barwani, I was told to go to Sendhwa, which had a history of communal riots behind it. True to expectation, a riot did break out at Sendhwa, the very last post of MP bordering Maharashtra. The place was notorious for communal outbreaks between sections of both Hindus and Muslims. On the day of Anant Chaturdashi, a huge traditional procession of Hindus was taken out through the streets. The SP of Barwani, Sri Chandorkar was camping at Sendhwa, looking into the sensitivities of the area. Peace keeping committee meetings had already been held.

On the day of the festival, a country made bomb was thrown on the unsuspecting Hindu crowds, from the top of a building. There was complete chaos. More militant among the Hindus openly raised slogans that they would burn down the Muslim houses and mohallas. Alarm bells of an imminent large scale riot were clearly heard. By now, fire balls soaked in petrol were freely thrown around. My jeep got stuck in a nallah at the very site where fire balls were being thrown. Some people pulled the jeep out of the nallah on the road. The SDO(P), Sri Shivhare insisted that a firing order must be given right away to avert a free for all. I signed the order in the jeep. There was no time for cool thinking. To save the town from a major communal holocaust, the shoot at sight order appeared imperative. Two persons died in the process.

Perhaps a major tragedy was averted. Curfew was clamped. The Divisional Commissioner Sri VN Kaul and IGP Sri Puri visited the spot next day. I still remember the deep set eyes of Sri Kaul, which kept on focusing on me from time to time. I would look furtively in other direction, averting his looks. I was in such a turmoil that I could not make out correctly what was happening. I was just swept off my feet by the events. The benign and cool handling of the situation by the DM Sri RN Berwa, saved the day. He was sympathetic. It turned out that there was a complete failure of intelligence. Later a magisterial inquiry was instituted by the DM. The enquiry concluded that timely action saved the day from a major disaster. So, that was that. The incident gives me goose pimples when I recollect. It was indeed baptism by fire. I learnt that the glib talk of the police officers should be taken with more than a pinch of salt.

In 1984, Mrs Gandhi had been assassinated and ripples were felt in Barwani also. The local MLA, Kanti Lal Bhuria attempted a large scale trouble. He organized a huge procession at the local thana and threatened to burn it. The situation was brought under control with his arrest and imposition of Section 144 under the Cr.P.C.

1. Alirajpur

I was transferred to Alirajpur, a sub division of the neighbouring Jhabua district. This was the hard core area of the so called criminal tribes of Bhils and Bhilalas. All red light vehicles were waylaid by them in the night and attacked. Police vehicles bore the major brunt. Fortunately no such incident occurred in my tenure. I remember the big patches of green forests in Alirajpur, in a surrounding sea of desert of Jhabua district.

Bhils are known for their honesty. If they commit a crime, they immediately confess next day, in the thana. By psyche, they cannot carry guilt in their conscience.

Alirajpur is the famed land of Bhagoria festival during Holi time. The bhil boys and girls dance to their drums and cymbols, daylong and night long. Their dresses are multicoloured and gorgeous. Men wear a turban and a lungi. Females dressed in saris and jewellery. They all dance including the visitors with abandon, under the influence of 'tadi'. In the process of festivity, they choose their wives/husbands, without fear or coercion. Energy of the youthful dancers is inexhaustible. Tadi, the local fermented drink of coconut palm flows freely. When freshly fermented, there is no bitterness in the drink, it is in fact sweet and pleasant. The ceremony of the Bhils is akin to the ghotul practice of Bastar. People from the world over, come to witness the colourful festival.

In 1984, Mr Rajiv Gandhi had become the Prime Minister of the country. He with his wife Sonia Gandhi, visited Alirajpur to study, interact and talk with the Bhils at the first hand. He himself drove the jeep through the dusty WBM roads. He witnessed how the bhils climbed up the coconut trees like a monkey, how they made cuts in the bark and collected juice and fermented their traditional country drink. Rajiv and Sonia Gandhi watched with glee at the entire operation and took a taste of the heady brew, profferred to them. Rajiv Gandhi was handsome, with infinite grace and a sense of joyful participation. He observed the famed bow and arrow skill of the Bhils as well. For the Bhils a bara babu had come from Delhi. There was something hypnotic in Rajiv Gandhi's grace, demeanour and the bewitching smile, which could not, but charm the others. Sonia Gandhi, a woman of few words, but with ready smile, followed him like a shadow. The trip was short but charming and memorable. All the endless recci trips and drills were successfully completed, and the trip ended, with a sigh of relief for us.

2. Dharamjaigarh

From Alirajpur, on the western margin of the state, I was shifted to the other extreme, the eastern border, to the region of Raigarh, now in Chhatisgarh. I was made the Project Officer of ITDP for the development issues of the tribals of the region like Gonds, etc. The project mainly pumped money for educational uplift and building of hostels and ashrams.

The area was indeed beautiful – with the stately sal and teak forests, and mahua, bahera and harra trees. There were jamuns, chironji and jackfruits in season. Tomato was grown in Lureg and so much was cultivated that it sold at 25 paise a kilo. Traders and middlemen purchased them for making high-end ketchups and pastes. The valued chironji was sold against a barter with common salt by the unscrupulous traders. Weekly supplies were ensured through mobile PDS shops at the hat bazaars of the tribals. It was a different world altogether.

The onset of winters tumbled the mercury from 40 to sub zero level. Fields and fields were loaded with endless mustard blossoms. The hilly, undulating landscape rightly gave it the epithet of 'Switzerland of India'.

The beautiful vales of Sisgringa Ghat and Jashpurnagar left one speechless, in the awed presence and admiration of the hallowed Nature. The stately sal and teak clothed the mountains and hills. There was an ancient site of rocky hills that still carried prehistoric rock paintings of the yore. Caves were used by the ancient Jain and Buddhist monks and other dwellers.

I was posted as the District Collector in three districts, one after the other – Sidhi, Damoh and Surguja, in a period of next five years.

Sidhi

Sidhi was located on the banks of two rivers Gopad and Banas. Population of the town was only 20,000 odd. The reason for the fame of the district was the small tehsil called Churhat, the constituency of Sri Arjun Singh and now of his son Rahul Singh.

When I joined, Arjun Singh had become the Governor of Punjab, but it was said that he still held the sway in state politics, especially in the affairs of Sidhi. I had chance to meet him twice only. On the first occasion, he held a meeting at the circuit house, a beautifully selected location on the top of a hill. He had selected the site himself and one must say it was impeccable. He had come to finalise the location of Navodaya Vidyalaya. The scheme had been just launched. I keenly observed the man and his reactions. He listened to all officers present. Then he asked the SDM to show the map of the district. He put his finger on a hill as the suitable site, which I felt was a good choice. The man had a great aesthetic sense.

The other occasion of encounter with him was when he was departing from the district. I and SP followed him in the carcade. When the boundary of the district was reached, we were supposed to get down and bid farewell to him. While we were in the process of getting down, we saw him getting down his car and coming towards us. He shook hands with us and went back to his car and went on his way forward. I was surprised by his show of courtesy.

Where was the rough behavior he was known for? I wished I had more meetings with him. But that was the last.

The officers ran scared of Sri Arjun Singh. When he took his meetings in the circuit house of Sidhi, he would go through the petitions of the general public, presented to him in earlier visits. He went through the action taken reports. It was famed that if he lifted his face from the papers, or if he adjusted his spectacles to look at the concerned officer, he could very well expect his marching orders in a day or two.

I had a fascination for natural rocks and old stone statues that were bestrewn throughout the region. A 'Kala Vithika' was set up to display them. Sri Moti Lal Vora inaugurated it, as he had taken over the reigns from Arjun Singh, who had been awarded a more prestigious assignment as Governor of Punjab by Mrs Indira Gandhi.

Sidhi is also famed for the black buck sanctuary, named after Sanjay Gandhi. The road upto the sanctuary at that time was non-existent. A rugged four wheel jeep was essential to negotiate the climb. On reaching up, we saw the stately black bucks in hordes. They sailed past us with the grace of a swan, then stopped, looked back at us and concluded that we were no threat to them. So, unhurriedly they carried on with their grazing with complete disdain of us.

Damoh

Damoh is known for the vast number of the Jain communities and their sacred shrines at Kundalgiri. There was also a holiest of the holy temple of Lord Shiva at Bandakpur, visited by the devotees in festivities.

The politics of the district was dominated by the Congress doyen, Bappa Tandon and after his death, by his son Anil Tandon. The leadership is now taken over by the BJP.

I collected old statues and relics, which were being stolen, from different parts of the district and put them together in a museum, created in the fortress like old building which housed the tehsil. This was tastefully renovated. It was inaugurated by Her Excellency the Governor of the State, Smt. Sarla Grewal.

The Collector's Bungalow was very huge, renovated by me in parts, laid with black marble. Old water bodies were preserved with some effort on my part.

I remember there was a tank in the garden of the Collector, which was used for watering. It was big enough to allow some swimming strokes. While I swam once, to my horror, I saw a big black snake in the water, swimming with me. Stricken with terror, I quickly came out of the tank, never to venture in again.

Surguja

Surguja was an erstwhile royal state of Sri MS Singhdeo and his forefathers, who was Chief Secretary of the state as well. It was a predominantly a tribal district, very huge in size. From end to end, it measured more than 200 kms.

The Naxalite and Peoples' Movement activities had begun to surface in areas adjoining Bihar. The main town was Ambikapur.

I remember with fondness the hill tract of Mainpat, which was earmarked and given to the Tibetan refugees for their rehabilitation. The place is cooler by at least 5 or 6 degrees compared with the surrounding areas. The displaced Tibetans make excellent carpets, valued by all.

The farmers grow buck wheat as a staple. Sri RP Kapoor once visited the area on a chopper. His wife and Mrs RV Gupta had to be brought by the chopper to Mainpat. Who would know the terrain from the air? The collector of course! So I was chosen to accompany them. I was full of trepidation. How would I identify the destination from the air? Without the foggiest idea, I rode the chopper with my esteemed guests. The pilot was as confused as us, about the landing place. After much dithering, he decided to land. I did not have a clue about where we were landing. Fortunately, as we landed, I saw the poor patwari reaching towards us. I heaved a big sigh of relief. My reputation for knowing the terrain grew up in others' estimate. I could only thank my stars and the patwari for making the fortuitous entry and thus saving the day for me.

I was posted as a Deputy Secretary in the Ministry of Welfare in the GOI. I was given the charge of Handicapped Welfare desk. I was able to watch the programmes run by NGO's for the handicapped people all across the country. I was able to go to almost all states. I must say that I was touched by the sincerity with which these programmes were run. Ngo's were generally, not the fly by night operators. The handicapped sector is in any case not easy. Without a modicum of dedication it was impossible to handle physical, visual, hearing, and mental disability. Dealing with disabled persons required care and affection. On many occasions I found that heads of the NGO's had a handicapped child in the family, which motivated them to a life of service and added a personal element in their approach.

My son was born while I was in Delhi, in 1992. A peaceful face, lovely eyes and lips, he looked like the Buddha. He grew up in Delhi, in initial years. He referred to himself in the third person and called himself 'bhaiya'. He was the darling of everyone at both paternal and maternal homes. Later he studied in Bhopal, completed his Mechanical Engineering from BITS Pilani, and he is currently doing Ph.d, in the University of Illinois near Chicago, USA.

Overseas

From the GOI, I got the opportunity to study at the Exeter University, UK, to do MBA in the Public Sector Management, under the Colombo Plan. A meagre stipend of 480 pounds a month was given. This meant that Nishi too had to work part time. We lived at Long Brook Street. 400 pounds was spent every month on the house rent. The rest was spent on food, which was comparatively cheap in the superstores.

Exeter was a beautiful city. It was a quayside town which was actually a popular holiday resort in the UK. We toured all tourist place of the country, on the weekends – London, Edinborough, Scotland, Shropshire, Canterbury, Bath,

Cardiff, etc.

The tour of Europe on a Youth Hostel accommodation basis, was done on a shoe string budget, for the duration of about ten days in the Easter break.

Our son Siddhansh was about 2 or 3 years at the time. It was a quirky age when the child logic and insistence, weighs supreme. He was a toddler. So he, as well as the luggage, had to be carried by us in person. Being tired, he usually refused to even walk. Of course there was no affordable porter system there and taxis were out of reach. He was fascinated by the trains, and would spend hours fiddling with the toy trains, at 'Early Learning Centre' in the High Street of Exeter.

We travelled extensively in Europe and saw Paris, Nice, Luxembourg, Brussels, Bruges, Rome, Venice, Florence, Vienna, Salzburg, Munich, Heidelburg, Zurich, Lake Lucerne, Prague, etc. I remember the sheer boisterousness of Prague, its medieval castles and Charles Bridge, the magnificence of St Peters Church of Rome, the unsurpassed beauty of Mona Lisa by Leonardo da Vinci, the grace of the Vatican, the awesome paintings of Michaelangelo in the ceilings of Sistine Chapel, the lifelike statue of David in Florence sculpted by Michaelangelo, the gondola ride in Venice (I found the city a bit decrepit, decaying and overrated), Champs de Elysees of the magical Paris, the incomparable and inexhaustible treasure of art at the Louvre, the langorous beauty of the sea resort of Nice, the bewitching Middle Age ambience of Bruges with the flowering daffodils and irises, the hallowed city of Mozart and Beethoven, Salzburg, the dominating alleys and waterways of Venice, the grandeur and beauty of the Catharine-Hapsburg empire of Austria, the massive forts and medieval palaces of Vienna, the old world charm of Heidelbourg in Germany, the gorgeous Van Gogh expressionistic paintings in the Ritz Museum of Amsterdam, the rows and rows of tulips in Keukenhoff garden, the huge windmills of Amsterdam, etc.

The system of pickups and drops at the various youth hostels was faultless, and it worked on the basis of advance reservations. People enjoyed and loved life to the hilt, their attitude to us always courteous and helpful. The fact that we were able to tour the entire continent without a single hiccup speaks volumes of the systems set up by the Europeans. There was no barrier of language, caste, creed or colour. It was indeed a grand tour de force of the European culture.

With the extended summer that year in Europe, called the Indian summer, my university campus transformed into a sort of beach-side resort for the students of the campus, who enjoyed the, balming sun in bikinis, in the gardens and in the pool.

I will never forget the heady fragrance of the honeysuckle flowers which had blossomed that time in the campus. The smell was so intense, that it entered the soul. I remember I would take long whiffs when I passed the bush. Morning strolls in the campus were unsurpassed nature walks. The myriad flora and fauna left me bewildered and breathless, especially the wild flowers. I did not mind the cold. Once the sun was out, it was a paradise on earth.

Classes in the university were a bit dull and listless and I must say a repetition of what I had already studied in India. We were three fellow Indians from IAS, from different cadres, Sri Saharia from Maharashtra, Sri Prem Narayan from UP and me. Teachers were uncomfortable with us. They dreaded us and our questions. They felt that we were either testing their knowledge or pulling their legs. We and our families were the kindred souls in the foreign country. Our get-togethers and jaunts to the Tesco's or the Sainsbury's were fun. It was an eye-opening introduction to the consumer world of the West to us.

Other postings

I served in different positions in the GOI and the Government of

Madhya Pradesh as Additional Chief Secretary in Rural and Cottage Industries Department, comprising of five sectors: Khadi & Village Industries Board Handloom Directorate Sericulture Board Handlooms & Handicrafts Board

Matikala Board (terracotta) Mining department, PHED, Etc, etc.,

I retired from professional commitments in June, 2016. The official status of retirement brought an end to a long and beautiful journey…

I remember Sri Sumit Bose and his lovely wife, Chandra Bose for their hospitality, gushing nature and kindness.

I remember with fondness Sri RN Berwa, Collector at Khargone and Sri Gopalakrishnan, Collector at Jhabua.

I remember the delightful time we had with Mr Rajan Katoch and family at Bilaspur.

Sri Prashant Mehta, at Academy of Administration was a smiling support for me at all times.

I cannot forget Mrs Alka Sirohi who despite her biting tongue, always supported me in difficult times.

Mrs Ivy Chahal was a dear boss, brimming with new ideas and innovations.

I cannot forget Mr IS Dani for his quiet cool dealings.

Last but not least, Mr Antony Desa was always a pillar of strength to me, as the Chief Secretary of the state.

Overall reflections on Bureaucracy

Bureaucracy of the older genre and type is more or less dead. One has to be on the alert, what people are whispering behind your back. Colleagues sometimes victimize you for small slights or for money. Important positions are meant for colleagues who are pliant or are politically acceptable. We are in for difficult times, throughout the country.

Gone are the days when a contrary note by an officer put the Chief Minister too in a difficult position. Now notes are prepared after consultation with the powers. Ministers expect exact compliances to their order. They take an unearthly interest in transfers and postings. Money is an important consideration at all levels.

Some unsaid truths about the IAS:

These are the assumptions an IAS officer lives with, and the reality therein.

We are in this service to serve. The truth is, we scarcely behave as servants.

We handle vast sums of money and human resourc es; we do not possess any ex- pertise for this task. We are not trained accordingly.

We have a very high opi nion of ourselves and our "intelligence" and "expe- rience", and think people respect us for what we are.. In reality, people genuflect before us due to the power we wield to either do benefit or damage.

Over the years we have de veloped the tendency to dis- tribute largesse, whether in kind or in ideas. We do not own what we distribute.

We are paid to manage things efficiently and create systems. In actuality, we thrive on mismanagement and chaos because that gives us the power to choose some over others.

We are supposedly the steel frame. In reality, we have no long-term vision. We take ad hoc decisions, look- ing to what the authority above us wants.

We exploit the system for preferential treatment-for ourselves and people known to us. We are hypocritical enough to say we do it to "help" people.

We know if we create sys- tems where everyone has ea sy access to services, we shall become superfluous. So we let things be.

We love to expand and en- hance our sphere of work. We do not bother to place systems to bring in the need- ed efficiency.

Worst of all, we are the most pompous, officious and ill-bred set of people. And we have the nerve to say we work for the people of this country.

In reality we have no stakes in this country - our children often study abroad and we have created a niche cocoon of the luxuries this system can give us.

We have no empathy with the larger populace, though we are always careful to make the right noises.

If there were any justice, we would have long been ex- tinct. But we are too power- ful to let ourselves be annihilated.

We are the IAS.

Interests and hobbies

I had formed an informal group of friends and interested persons, who met once in a fortnight, to talk and discuss about the various aspects of yoga, meditation and spirituality. The group met regularly over tea/coffee at my place.

But life in civil service is not the end in itself. Whatever one feels one has achieved, is ephemeral. It may engage us for some time. It may even lead us to interlace our conversations with, 'when I was posted in district blah blah blah', for a life time. Life is all around us – not in some halfforgotten memoirs.

I have tried to pursue a other interests over the years. I list them here:

1. Travelling
2. Photography
3. Painting
4. Reading
5. Writing
6. Meditation practices

And some physical fitness...

The gym bug bit me, quite early, when I was in the graduate class. The gyms at that time were abominable.

In the Mussoorie Academy, people were engrossed in forging new friendships. I would do my bit for half an hour in the gym.

In the earlier postings, transfers were too frequent for me to fall into a gym discipline. Only after Bhopal, I have a semblance of a settled life, and I am able to do the exercises on a regular basis.

I find the yogic asanas and exercises too undemanding and slow. They are indeed good for correcting ailments and as a regular, preventive, long term regime. Indeed pranayam is the doorway to meditation. But as a form of physical exercise, yogic asanas are not my cup of tea. I like weights in a gym.

Yoga

To understand yoga, I did a diploma course on yogic sciences from Barkatullah University, Bhopal. Patanjali's Ashtanga Yoga is spoken of in hallowed tones. But Patanjali was writing in different times and milieu, and for the adept sages and rishis. He emphasised the meditative aspects mostly. But today there are hordes and hordes of centres that dish out different variations of yoga - dynamic and pilate, bordering on aerobic exercises, as if they are an end in themselves, under the brand name of 'yoga', especially for the gullible westerners. We even celebrate an 'International Yoga Day', now, on 21st June, to impress upon the world that we are the originators of yoga.

Therefore it cannot be said that we have a monopolistic right over its heritage. We cannot lay claim to cultural heritage for things bequeathed from remote antiquity. At best, it is a world heritage, with origin from India.

Art and culture...

Leonard Bernstein said, it's the artists, and the thinkers who will, ultimately save us, who can articulate, educate, defy, insist, sing and shout the big dreams.

My interest in art and painting has sustained over a long period of time. It began with water colors. I have been dabbling in water colours for the last twenty years. I picked up the hobby somehow – possibly natural inclination. I am a self-taught artist, without a formal training. Now I do water colours, acrylics and oil colours.

In painting I have found my vocation. I paint on the subject of NATURE - mountains, rivers, trees, flowers, seaside, etc. Art enables me to express my passion. The study of development of Western art as one continuous movement is fascinating. From classical Greek and Roman, to the modern Abstracts, it is one development, from beginning to end, led by artists and schools.

I am fascinated by **theImpressionists and the Expressionist schools.**

The works of **Raphael, Velasquez, Manet, Monet, Cezanne, Pissaro, Van**

Gough, Picasso, Gauguin, among others, at the Louvre of Paris, the Tate Art Gallery of the UK, Rikz and Van Gough Museums of the Netherlands, the Chicago National Museum, and the supremely magnificent Pushkin National Museum are unparalleled collections of art enthusiasts. one ponders on how much store the people of these countries lay on art. Art heritage is part of their treasure, something to live by, and to teach the younger generation about.

NGMA's of Delhi and Mumbai house a huge collection of Indian artists like Raja Ravi Verma, Raza, Souza, Amrita Sher Gill, Prabha, Jamini Roy, the Bengal School, etc. They have found an honorable place in the world art scene!

I have held solo exhibitions of my works in the art galleries across the country.

Some prominent ones are:

Jahangir Art Gallery, Mumbai - considered the Mecca of art in India

Lalit Kala Academy, Delhi, Lalit Kala Academy, Lucknow Bharat Bhawan, Bhopal, which hosts national and international art and culture shows.

CSOI Gallery, Delhi, dedicated to the art efforts of bureaucrats and their spouses.

Pritam Lal Dua Art Gallery Indore

Kala Vithika Gwalior

Rani Durgavati Art Gallery Jabalpur

Gallery of the Cabinet Secretariat Delhi.

Kalakriti Art Gallery, Hyderabad.

India Habitat Centre, Delhi.

Art and artists in India are in a dismal state.

Photography

I have travelled extensively through the country and abroad. A photography exhibition was held by me at Indira

Gandhi Manav Sangrahalaya, Bhopal, 'THE MUSEUM OF MAN'. At present they are on display at the Noronha Academy of Administration, Bhopal.

The most important element of photography is composition of the subject. What to include and what to avoid in the frame makes all the difference. This happens instinctively. With the digital revolution, it is easy to edit the photographs. Moreover, the cost of the film roll is no longer a consideration, with the availability of unlimited digital space. Importance of the morning light and the golden hour of the evening are crucial to good photography.

Photobook enhancing and editing has brought in a new dimension to photography.

Reading

Pre-history: Need for a new look at our ancient past

My interest in human prehistory is abiding. There was at one time an advanced civilisation, which was destroyed by the natural upheavels and cataclysms. **Erich Von Daniken earlier, and Graham Hancock** currently, fill me with awe and fascination. I have read all books of both authors. To go further, there **are geologists/archaelogists like Robert Bauval, Randall, Anthony West and Robert Schoch who have painstakingly researched and investigated the past events and built up a formidable literature on the subject.**

The studies are not all in the air, figments of someone's fantasy. They are well documented and authenticated. Perhaps there was a lost civilisation, perhaps there was an advanced technology, perhaps the aliens visited us. We do not know who we are because we have failed to go to our own roots, to the ancient past. Truth may be hidden in the depths of the earth, sea and space. We cannot remain satisfied with gradualism or evolutionism of **Darwin.** There may have been unusual events in the past far beyond human capabilities. We need to study layer after layer of the earth, the rocks, the glaciers, the polar ice caps to uncover the story. The outer space is still undiscovered. It is a fact that a 150 square feet massive asteroid piece hit and devastated Siberia in 1 08, in Tunguska.

It is documented that a massive hit by an asteroid or a comet, much larger than what hit Siberia around twelve thousand years back, had hit the earth and had brought about a devastation that changed everything on earth. Plato gives 11600 BC for the date for the cataclysm, that led to the submergence of Atlantis. It also triggered the last Ice Age.

Again around nine thousand years ago, there was again an unusual collision that led to a sudden warming of the earth, the glacial melt, the world wide flood, massive climate upheaval, the filling of the continental shelves around the world – the end of Ice Age. It was the result of another asteroid impact. Impact event is narrated by all folklores and ancient civilisations. Impact studies are documented and they show the formation of nano diamonds in Asian European continents. The location of the impact crater is still elusive, but believed to be somewhere in the miles deep glaciers of North America, still to be located.

The alternative study of **Robert Schoch** shows that extraordinary sun activity in its corona, sent massive coronal streams from the centre of the sun to the earth, which caused electrical currents, fields and auroras to be generated in massive land areas like Cappaducia in Turkey and some caves in India. These led to unusual scarrings.

The unravelled mysteries are pointers to what more may be in store to be discovered.

Our main theme of the book of self-discovery, cannot be answered fully, unless we investigate our ancient past, our own human genealogy, our racial origin and understand the ancient earth events.

travels in India and across the globe…

Journeys, long and short, by rail, road, air or water, leave a deep impression. Being a Gemini, the air sign, I love the periodical breaks from the humdrum.

It has been commented that journeys should actually take you forward. Sometimes, we may be travelling to far distances, but our minds remain entrenched in the past worries. Journeys should enable us to break free from our problems, to see new lands and to meet new people. Otherwise we remain saddled with our baggage, and oftentimes, we heave a sigh of relief when we return – a complete travesty and wastage.

Travel by **road** in a car is like travelling in the familiarity of home. The thrill of adventure of the unknown is missed. It is like seeing new places from the safety of the windows of home.

Train journey is a different kettle of fish. You sit in an anonymous seat surrounded by a sea of people. All are immersed in their own thoughts. Some people are garrulous, some are quiet, some hide behind a book. The monster train hurtles through the changing landscape at a great speed. Summer landscape is dry and parched, fields barren and trees without a single leaf. It is as if someone has personally torched the trees and set them on fire. We zip past the summer landscape, sitting in the cool comfort of an AC compartment. The outside terrain changes, hilly, rocky and forested, undulating and littered with nullahs and small dried up river paths. The train, unmindful of the rough terrain, continues smoothly. It passes through a sudden open chasm or sometimes a river rushes underneath. The feeling is as if the ground has slipped under the feet. Exhilarating! I have often had a childish nightmare of the train, falling headlong in a deep chasm of water. The dream never fails to scare me.

Another joy of a train travel is that one can settle down and have a quiet read of a book, over sips of ginger tea and biscuits. With the onset of drowsiness, one falls to a slumber to the clitter clatter of the train.

Air travel is quick and eventless. The only drama is at take-off and landing.The variety of people and places encountered during a train travel is absent in an air ride.

One is confined, at the beck and call of the hostesses.

Travel by the sea is usually exciting. But the initial enthusiasm wanes as one embarks on the placid journey. The endless sea all around and the wobble of the carrier leads many to sea sickness. I had undertaken the voyage from Chennai to Port Blair, a little staid.

Mumbai to Diu was a different kettle of fish. With a rollicking marriage party to boots. The untramelled views of the sunrise and the moon rise were like balm to the spirit.

The open decl takes care of walks. The gym for exercises.

The variety of foods and cuisines are a foodies's delight. Continental, Italian, Mexican, chat, Indian, Jain – you think of it and it is there. The experience is of a super luxury travelling hotel.It is never eventless and boring! To top it all, there is a pool and a DJ and non-stop music and dance for all to participate. A Bohemian Rhapsody!

Some travel memories that bring me back to my search for answers...

Memories are the repertoire of sensations and experiences. Mind is like a lamp which lights up the area of consciousness focussed upon.

I would attempt to draw from my store of memories, as far as specific journeys are concerned. IAS officers get innumerable opportunities to travel, inland and overseas. This happens as official trips, LTC's and as holidays.

When I think of **Wynad**, the thickly forested area of God's own country, Kerala, I vividly remember the coconuts, the oil palms, the areca plantations, etc, in endless stretches. I cannot forget the enchanted coffee blossoms on both sides of the hill road. White flowers loaded the coffee bushes. The whole area smelled sweeter and headier than jasmine. I had a delightful half hour in the magic fairyland.

I have travelled extensively **in Kerala**. Who would not fall in love with God's own country? I went **to Mahi**, a small constituency, surrounded by the territory of Kerala. Historically, Mahi was a port of Portuguese settlement. I would watch the massive sea beach from my window. There was a light house adjoining the circuit house which gave a superb panoramic view of the sea.

Somewhere in this sprawling beach, in the 16th century, Vasco da Gama had set his anchor to the Indian shore. Kalaripatu, the most ancient martial art of India, originates from here. Shaolin tradition of China was an offshoot of this tradition. The martial art required agility of mind and limbs and a close coordination between them. I took some training lessons in the art as fun, but even the first steps with the bamboo stick were difficult.

I went to **Alleppey**, the alluring backwaters, Thekkadi Wild

LIfe sanctuary, the Chinese fishing nets at Cochin, Munnar Tea Estate and of course Trivandrum. I visited the Kerala Ayurvedic Vaidyashala at Kottayam.

Goa is truly the fun city of India. It is strewn with magical

Palm laden beaches – Calangute, Colva, Baga, Anjuna, Varca, Miramar and so on. Bohemian care free life is the DNA of Goa. Food and beer served in the shacks is real joy. Of all, I loved Baga, for its vibrance and joi de vivre.

Mumbai, the maximum city, the city that never sleeps, has all possible fun, food and entertainment. I remember my excitement when I first touched the waters of the Chowpatty Beach. Mumbai is a great fashion centre.

Bollywood, big Malls and stores all go hand in hand.

Dharmendra and Mumtaz were shooting for 'Loafer' at that time, and we sat for hours watching them. Maratha Mandir was screening Sambandh, which we saw and enjoyed. We stayed at Nataraj Hotel, on the Marine Drive. This was way back in early seventies. Afterwards I went to the city countless times.

There is nothing like **Lakshdweep Island** in India. The flight lands at Kavaratti Airport, which is an extension into the sea on both sides. The sight of the white sands blows you. To walk on the white beach, in the early glow of the rising sun is out of the world. Not a soul disturbs you. Palm trees sway, little birds begin their morning cahoots, and you can live in the lap of nature in complete silence for an hour or the whole day. You can palpably sense the divine presence. Just you and nature and divine energy. What more!!

We spent glorious four days in the Island. Waves ebbed and flowed in a cadence reminding of Matthew Arnold, Break, break, break, N thy cold grey stones sea !

What was heard by Sophocles at the Aegean Sea ages ago, is repeated by nature day in and day out, in this ethereal place. We spent hours at the lazy beach – nothing else to do.

Bangaram Island is of course a jewel, shaped like a ladies necklace. The beach is cosy and safe as a home pool. You could fun and frolic with the waves, and the gentle breeze for hours. My son, Siddhansh, who had picked up all the tricks of the camera, tried his hand at the glorious bounties of nature thrown about us in abandon. The gentle boat that brought us here, took us back to Kavaratti. We took the fight next day to the mainland, bidding adieu and resolving to come back again.

Andaman and Nicobar Islands, on the other side of the Deccan, is more frequented and better organised. **Port Blair** is a big airport. We were lodged in a beautiful Guest House with a view of the mighty Bay of Bengal. There are so many hidden jewels in the Island.

The vandoor beach was swallowed up by the last tsunami and what is left is not even half of the original. **Mayabundar** is now inaccessible.

Ross Island and **the Cellular Jail** are steeped in the

British history of a troubling period.

We cannot forget the little **Corbyn's Cove** beach, which is again full of tourists and it is virtually a hawkers' delight – coconuts, ice creams, mangoes, pakoras, tea, and all the stuff.

The **North Island** is meant for water sports like scuba diving, snorkelling, speed boats, etc.

Kaala Pathar is a great beach for sea bath with the swells of gigantic waves, literally taking you deep inside and throwing you up again.

Radha Nagar Beach in the Havelock Island, is tom tommed as the best beach in the world.

The shining jewel is the Neil Island, which has a phenomenal natural gate, sculpted by the waves in the rocky coast.

The haunt of the Jaravas is reached after restricted passage through one of the best preserved rain forest of the world. The variety of palms and the vegetation literally overwhelms you with its beauty.

I recall the mist laden foliage of **Gangtok,** in Sikkim, with fern filled hillsides of all varieties. The early morning walks were an invitation to daily discoveries and adventures. I was especially enamoured by the strange fragrance of those mist laden hillside flowers and foliage, peculiar to the mountain air.

The morning walks in **Dharamshala** hills were enchanting. At 5.30 in the morning, when there were just tweaks of light in the sky, it was a great pleasure to saunter past the mighty pine and deodar trees. Chill and pine fragrance pervaded the air. The wild roses, the jacarandas, the apricot blossoms almost hid the snow peaks of **Dhauladhar** in the background. The beautiful rare bird, monal, is sighted when the bird is unaware of the trespasser in its territory. Reaction in the alert bird is sudden and electric. And it would fly away at the slightest smell of danger. Indeed its wing span is eight feet. It is the stae bird of Himachal Pradesh.

The rising mists in the valley, and the peeping sun through the fog were all a heady concoction and a subject for a landscape artist. After an hour of walk, back to the Circuit House, I would sit in my glass house room with a 360 degree view of the Dhauladhar, and enjoy the sips of the delectable local leaf tea, from the nearby Mann Tea Estate, which rivalled the Darjeeling tea with its crisp flavour. It was my cup of inebriation. It was sheer magic.

I took the trek to **Triund** which was about thirty kilometres. It was a popular trek with the local people. The sheer sight of the magical snow as one progressed and as it drew closer, was exhilarating. Negotiation of the mountain path is itself tricky and dangerous. But in the end it was a satisfying experience.

I had the first experience of water sports and skiing at **Pedong** lake. I fell so many times in the cool water as I took the lessons.

I took lessons in para gliding at **Bir/Billing**, a mountain peak with a sheer fall into the valley, apt for the sport. It is characterised as the best site for paragliding in the country. Paratroopers from Holland and other European destinations could be seen filling the sky. It looked so daunting and dangerous to take those first steps into abyss. But conquering the initial fear, once air borne, there is a sense of release and oomph. Light headed and giddy, you start to enjoy the thrill of the avian world, where one is kept aloft by the wind. I could see snow peaks from the heights.

I went to **Shoja,** forty kilometres off Kullu. It is a hidden gem amidst the green coniferous forests. From the forest lodge, there is a mountain trek through the verdant hills. The kachcha walkway is laden with fresh coniferous and chestnut leaves and cones. In season wild iris cover the side ways end to end. A few yellow daffodifs smile in the ocean of blue of the iris. A cool crisp wind through the distant vistas wraps you. You get drunk with the mountain magic. Its completely secluded from human presence. You feel so alone, surrounded by nature. It is a virtual heaven! A page from **Thoreau's 'Walden'.** The place has stuck in my memory as one of the most beautiful place on earth.

I remember the beautiful **Udupi** beach and its wild waves that struck with violence, rolled back and struck again with a mightier force. The pristine beach was indeed out of the world. I enjoyed the lazy hour of play with the waves, and the warm salty sea water, which tingled the skin.

Temple darshan in the south Indian tradition of a lungi was very calming, satisfying and fulfilling. Dosa and coffee in the roadside shops were just too good for the hungry stomach.

At **Chennai** I stayed at Taj Vivanta. I remember reading the book on 'Vipassana' by William Hart in one night, sitting in the verandah of my room, overlooking the sea. I realised the falseness of the sensations, emotions and thoughts. It was a profound awakening. I completed the book at 2 in the night, went to gym for exercise and a quick rejuvenating bath in the sea. I got a new insight into human frailties and some inkling of who I am not.

The wild barrenness of **Leh** desert narrates a beauty of its own. The sheer size and hues of the rocky terrain left one speechless. The deep cobalt blue of the Pangdong Lake, lined with snow peaks was a scene created by the wand of a wizard. And there was nothing to surpass the snow covered devastated barren beauty of the ZOZILLA Pass.

The newly laid out tulip garden in **Srinagar**, inaugurated by Mrs. Sonia Gandhi five years back is a testimony to the fact that be it a soft hearted poet or a hard hearted terrorist, the sense of beauty and its appreciation is a human trait. It unites all humanity. Rows and rows of yellow, red, pink, white and black tulips attract tourists from all parts of the country. The Kashmiri kahwa is sold in the garden by poor Kashmiri folks, savoured for its saffron, badam and elaichi flavour. It is poured out of the ornate metal containers and given in paper cups at the inexpensive rate of Rs 20 each. In that ambience and in that setting of tulip flowers, it is indeed an experience of the 'jannat'.

Jabalpur evokes the memory of a few million jugnus, the fireflies, which lighted up a dingy bush in our evening stroll in the university campus. The fireflies seemed to love lantana bushes, which they infested in huge numbers. It looked as if it was decorated with an endless number of burning candles. The spectacle was bewitching. I caught one of these fireflies in my palm, dreading that the fire would burn my palms. But it stopped glowing immediately and looked pathetic in captivity.

My grandfather, Sri Bishambhar Dayal, was the Chief Justice of Madhya Pradesh High Court in the mid seventies. When he was transferred from Allahabad High Court, the judicial officers were amazed that he carried a small trunk which carried all his belongings. He was a follower of Radha Swami group of Swami Bagh of Agra. He did satsang twice a day in which all satsangis of Jabalpur town participated. Thereafter, he sat for dhyan for two hours alone, in a dark chamber. He would expect all family members to sit with him at a simple dinner, which was prepared by my Naniji.

The residence of the Chief Justice was a sprawling bungalow surrounded by acres of land with mango and jamun trees. We used to go to Jabalpur in summer vacations. All my maternal cousins gathered and we had a ball of time. Rainfall used to be so heavy that all roofs and tin covers flooded with water, which rushed from the crevices and gargoyles like a gushing river. We used to have hours of bathing under these watery spouts. Mangoes and jamun quenched us with their mellow sweetness. The smell of mehndi and molsari flowers pervaded the garden. Night walks were ethereal and fill me with sweet remembrance even now.

We would go out to markets and cinemas and get stranded in the torrential rain more often than not. My Mama was married when Nanaji was in Jabalpur. The Indian Coffee House was a legend even then, and one of the best in central India. The sadar bazaar reminded me of the beautiful cantonment area of Allahabad. Indeed, the structure and habitation of the town was very similar to the newer areas of Allahabad. I can never forget the town of Jabalpur.

Udaipur is a royal city, the 'city of lakes' as is the popular name, strewn with medieval palaces and gardens. The lake Palace and the City Palace, with exquisite stonework and carvings, and treasures, are a medieval legacy. The spacious gardens, the courtyards and the boulevards are of royal proportions, a wonder of architectural design.

Visit to **Maharana Pratap**'s fortress at **Kumbalgarh** was awe inspiring. It was plain, stark and spartan, no frills at all. It was meant to house his army, the soldiers and the horses. on a high hill and surrounded by a rough terrain. **The Maharana** held his own against the Moghuls for long years. But the military history is strewn with victories and defeats, with palace intrigues, bloodbaths and unforgiving strains and tensions of the battles. His long reign brought peace to his people. But he was ultimately weakened by family intrigues.

Nath Dwara temple greeted us with closed doors as we had messed up the timing.

Cuisine of Rajasthan is unique. Delectable food items like 'choorma roti' 'gatta,' local herbs, 'chatni' are indeed mouth watering.

Bali is an important international tourist resort. The beaches, the temples, the people are loveable. We were fortunate in having a lovely companionship with Nellie and Pratimaji. The tour operators made a mess of the programme however and they thought we were interested only in shopping malls. We missed the more famous beaches and other tourist attractions like rice fields and shacks where Julia Roberts had shot '**Eat, pray and love**'.

I resolved to return again with son.

The trip to **Sri Lanka** was short and rewarding. Sri lankans are hardworking, fun loving, outgoing friendly people. Most of them have either a connection with India or have visited the country. The younger generation takes pride in completing their education in the UK, USA or India. While maintaining tradition, they have gone beyond. They love Western styles and adopt them willingly. The country is bestrewn with lovely places like Kandy, Nuwara Eliya, Galle, Colombo etc. The country assimilates the Tamil, British and Portuguese influences. Three major religions are prevalent- Hindus, Buddhists and Christians.

Kandy preserves the tooth relic of the Buddha.

Galle is a Portuguese remnant, steeped in this culture – people here love lazy days and sumptuous Portuguese meals, Streets are crammed with old style boutique sops, souvenirs, cafes, and pizzerias. A lovely sea lashes at its coast. In short, a lazy, sleepy, unhurried town with a lot of old historical monuments!

Bentota is a seaside resort with huge waves breaking on the rocks and the beaches.

Colombo is a gem of a town, with a beautiful coast, museums, markets and recreations. It is superior to Mumbai in many ways – civic amenities, well planned streets, cleanliness, huge corporate houses and of course the fun loving Sri Lankans.

The trip to **Egypt** was an experience which introduced me to one of the earliest cradles of civilisation. The pyramids, the temples of Karnak at luxor, and at Memphis , Hatshepsut, of osiris, the mighty Sphinx, the cruise down the Nile are treasured memories.

The Pyramids of Khufu, Khafre and Menkaure at the Giza Plateau, were visible from the room of Hotel Meena Palace, where we had stayed. There were other pyramids at Djoser and Saqqara which we visited. Pyramids are of course an enduring mystery and puzzle. The King's Valley stored innumerable tombs and mummies.

The legend of Osiris and Isis are the foundation stories of the Egyptian culture. The Cairo Museum gave a glimpse of the riches of **King Thutmose, Nefertiti, Amenhotep**.

The water at the swimming pool at Meena, was surprisingly cold and forbidding.

The Nile cruise organised by the oberoi's was an experience in ultimate luxury. We were completely to ourselves because other members had to join where we were to drop.

Anurag, Poonam and Raghu were with us. In fact Anurag had organised the trip. One learned so much about our wonderful past.

Australia and New Zealand, in the Down Under, were an introduction to a different kind of world and culture, now more or less free from the British legacy. My sister and brother in law, Anurag showed us all exotic and wonderful places. The Rotorua area is laden with sulphur springs and the Maories.

In Australia we went to Cairns and the **Great Barrier Reef**.

The Coral Reef is fragile now and it is protected as a World Heritage. **Brisbane** is a very beautiful city, well planned with all the trappings of city life. But the parks and open spaces are beautiful. **Gold Coast** is the most expensive property in the world.

Thailand, and Indonesia attract international tourists in hordes. They are cosmopolitan cultures with lovely beaches, markets and fun places. People are mostly Muslims, Buddhists, Hindus and Chinese. Barabodur is ancient and a wonder of the world.

Bhutan

Bhutan is a royal princely state, Buddhist in nature, with the highest happiness index. It's a little jewel with so many wonderful places, still in a state of medieval dream. We went to Thimphu and Paro. Tiger's nest, the famous monastery was accessible after a long and difficult, steep climb on the hill. I could not go up full height. I went only as far as the pony went. Nishi and others completed the whole climb.

Russia

A truncated state now, it was the largest at one time. The collapse of the Soviet Regime has no grievers now. The country is rich, mighty, and a part of the larger European culture. People are huge, healthy, ruddy and very courteous. In Moscow, we went to the Kremlin, St. Basil's Cathedral, St Paul's Cathedral and the National Museum and other galleries. The National Museum is a treasure house.

Food is served in large proportions in the various restaurants. The Russians eat and drink in generous quantities. Vodka is a popular, sparkling drink. An Indian restaurant, 'Tandoor' took care of our vegetarian palate. Russians are indeed big drinkers and voracious meat eaters. Raj Kapoor, Amitabh Bachchan and Mrs Indira Gandhi are remembered fondly.

From Moscow, I and Nishi went to St. Petersburg by train, an overnight journey. St Petersburg, earlier leningrad, was the home of the last royal sovereignty. King Nicholas II, of the Romanov Dynasty, and his family, were poignantly executed by the Bolsheviks in a treacherous manner. St. Petersburg is an art city. Pushkin Museum is one of the biggest I have seen anywhere. Peter Hof is a rich and opulent summer palace of the kings. Church of the Savior on Spilled Blood, the Hermitage are all very rich and huge. The predominant colour on almost all the buildings is the shining gold – gilded domes and steeples.

From San Francisco, we went for a trip to Hawaii Island and spent leisurely time at an Airbnb resort with Siddhansh and Lucille, and enjoyed the seaside life on the beaches.

Portait of my mother

Some travel pictures

Hyderabad art exhibition

Bhutaan

https://apis.mail.yahoo.com/ws/v3/mailboxes/@.id==Vj N-FafuJ1-

KOUo1Uk73BUjg209vHmucmAaZPPREnQyrmxUiGw8 w7R37HMJSFCtSDt1n6F67

6llwJijNHGM9Rx73ng/messages/@.id==ANY-

kkNAPmuaXr_KcgbxWM2gmAE/content/parts/@.id= =2/thumbnail?appId=YMailNo
rrin&downloadWhenThumbnailFails=true&p

The USA

A huge and magnificent country, a book can be written on America alone. Its geographical enormity and its varied physical landscape had always puzzled me. Study of the cataclysmic origin of the country is best given in Graham Hancock's book, 'America Before'and After- a book of natural devastation of Americas.

There are fifty American states that constitute the United States of America. The Americans were indeed the 'last men standing', by mid 1850ies with the exhaustion of Europe, the Japan and China. Russia was never in the capitalist game.

The American era had begun.

A month long trip is not enough to even begin to understand the country. It only whets the appetite to see more and more of the country

Rochester

From Chicago we took a three day trip to Rochester, which meant to night journey by train, particularly to see the Niagara Falls.

The great Lakes Michigan, Ontario are glacial melts. They contain one fifth of the Earth's freshwater.

Niagara falls, running east to west, are located on US and Canada border. They are only 167 feet high and drain about 4 million cubic feet of water per minute. Its age is estimated at about 14000 years old.

San Francisco

San Franciso, an hour's drive from San Jose, boasts of many lofty skyscrapers, well laid out straight streets and avenues, running from from east to west, through the length and breadth of the city. There is also a crooked street, where the road cannot be seen because of its crookedness.

We went to the **Golden Gate Bridge** in San Francisco.

The huge San Francisco Bay lies in the fault of San

Andreas with a peculiar semicircle shape along the Pacific Ocean. It is a mix of salt and fresh waters, where the rivers drain.

The **Golden Gate** emerges out of the blue through the surrounding clouds and mists. Golden red in colour, it is an engineering marvel, the manner in which piers were erected in the sea bed. To drive over the deep blue, expansive, distant Pacific Ocean, is exhilarating, to say the least.

Las Vegas

From San Jose we flew to Las Vegas. Las Vegas is located in the Red Rock country. Ancient limestones and recent sandstones intermix in the region.

Vegas is the famed gaming bowl of not only the USA but the entire world. It is crammed with casinos and gamble houses.

The Grand Canyon

The Grand Canyon is the most stunning and intriguing landscape in the USA.

It is comparatively, a baby in geological age. It was formed 7 to 6 million years ago, although its age is considered still indeterminate. It is a labyrinth of ravines, channels, water sheds and gorges. The Northern Rim is 8200 feet high while the South Rim is flat.

The Grand Canyon, with its hypnotic folds, of gold and red cliffs, is one of the most magnificent wonders of this planet. A mile deep, 18 miles wide and 277 miles long, it is hard to believe or appreciate unless it is seen. One can hike on the trails down the sandstone cliffs, raft in the Colorado River, or just stand on the rim wondering at the amazing sight. We took the south rim.

We drove for an hour from **Flagstaff** to reach it, the nearest town to it.

Geologists feel that the unsolved enigma of the Canyon persists.

Antelope Canyon

Antelope Canyon trip is nothing less than spectacular in the land of Navajo Indians in Page. The rock formations were scooped at the time of catastrophic land shifts and sea erosion. They are red, pink, yellow, in character with a rift valley. This Slot Canyon, with natural slots opening upto the sky, is the most photographed spot in America. Antelope Canyon is iconic, with underground chambers of twisting rock lit by the natural windows above the sky.

The **Horseshoe Bend** is another famous must-see spot in the area. The site begs to be photographed. The Colorado River loops around an enormous peninsula of vertical craggy rocks like a necklace. The view is surreal. The half mile trail in the hot sun to the Bend, intimidates many visitors. We gallantly braved the sun and the climb to be rewarded with a stunning view of the dramatic Bend. And one is intrigued by the rafters down below in the Colorado river negotiating the waters as an intrepid adventure.

Sedona

After a restful night at Flagstaff, the next morning we drove to Sedona, also called the Red Rock country. A landscape as wild and diverse as the Red Rock country, is amenable to many ways of exploration. There are jeep tours, helicopter tours, hot air balloon rides, horseback rides, etc.

We preferred our car ride.

Sedona's natural beauty and spiritual energy make it an ideal place to pursue wellness. The red rocks provide an incredible backdrop for a robust workout. Rocks are said to produce enormous vortex of energy at some places. It also boasts of nation's best healers. There are acupressure, reiki or Oigong kiosks, and salt rooms for halo therapy. For mental wellness one is offered classes in yoga, or mindfulness or hypnotherapy.

Urbana Champagne

My son Siddhansh is doing Ph.D in Mechanical

Engineering at the University of Illinois, at Urbana Champagne campus of the University. We stayed with him in his University accommodation for a week.

The American way of life

Americans have a short history as a nation, but they have established an unparalleled system of the rule of law. The citizens have respect for their history, forefathers and institutions. The right to life, liberty and private property are sacred and inviolable. It is indeed the bedrock of the US Constitution. The right is carried to an extreme length sometimes. Guns and firearms do not need license. The result is that shoot outs are frequent, reminiscent of the grim gun battles of the Wild West tradition. This is a dark aspect of the American life.

America is a land of dreams, of fulfilment, of free flow of ideas. The open society, the research tradition, the healthy peer debates, the freedom to introduce a new ideas and the readiness to accept refutations to it after deliberation, shows that the society is truly open. It values democracy and its liberal tradition.

Journey's end

I have walked through the journey of life as Alice in wonderland. Meaningless characters came and went leaving temporary imprints in the memory, nothing more. I have visited the holy shrines of **Kedarnath, Badrinath, Gangotri, Yamnotri, Jagannath Puri, Rameshwaram, Somnath, Dwarka, Jwala Devi, Vaishno Devi, Dakshineshwar, Belur, Vishwanath temple, Mahakal, great temples of the south etc etc. But this** kind of religious tourism was usually devoid of any spiritual content. It was religious voyeurism, nothing more. Poojas, aartis, and rituals do not lead to any deeper spirituality.

Five shrines areTunganath, Joshimath, Rudranath, Kalpeshmar, Madmaheshwar, Guptakashi, all over10000 ft in height.

The analogy is that of a rolling stone that gathers no moss. Nothing sticks. All joys and sadness, all misses and achievements are a mental, ephemeral phenomena, not permanent or real.

Can any kind of permanence be found in the transitory world? What is the meaning of all this?

Sartre, Camus , Nietzsche and the Western thought in general, believes in the existential reality. But without any deeper anchor, they are led to despair and nihilism.

Some personal moments of intense peace

I remember vividly an episode when I was about 8 years old. As was the practice, we would bring out our chairs in the garden in the winters, to soak the sun. In a state of half doze, I heard the far off cries of the crows and eagles. It appeared as if they were calling me by my name, 'Munna', beckoning me to join them. Perhaps I was connecting to some other dimension. An epiphenomenon?

On another occasion, while I was lying in my bed on a summer night under the open sky, the canopy of stars made my imagination run wild, took imaginary flights to the vast stellar spaces. It was a journey of a different kind. An intoxicated experience of higher consciousness!

Who then are we?

Nisargadutta says, there is a reality beyond 'I am', and distinguishes between false 'I' and true 'I'. He calls it 'para brahma', which cannot be understood by our human apparatus. Para brahma is non-existence; changeless and beyond our comprehension, beyond even consciousness. There is no path to it.

Shankaracharya, in his Vedanta philosophy, points to one reality, whose exact nature can never be grasped by the human faculties. Even the why and how of existence can never be known. All is a part of the great game of the divine 'leela'.

JK Krishnamurthy speaks of the choiceless awareness that confronts every individual, in his book, **'Freedom from the known'.**

The other explanation

The Quantum Theory, the 'String Theory', the 'Multiple

Universe' Theory, the 'Field Theory' have been postulated. Universe is energy. The 'Akashic Theory of **Ervin lazslo** goes on to say that even vacuum is surcharged with energy. Water energy patterns were studied by the Japanese scientist, **Masaru Emoto**.

The whole revolution was begun by Planck and **Einstein** who gave birth to the unruly child, the Quantum Theory, which no one has fully understood.

Planck and others showed that the photons are both particles and waves.Even matter is not solid, but a jumble of waves. The concept of entanglement confirmed Einstein's 'spooky action at a distance'. **Particles seemed to travel faster than light, the outer limit set by Einstein for speed.**

Ultimately both spiritual and scientific understandings come to the conclusion that reality is one consciousness is one, - which our rishis have been asserting for ages.

HUMAN DESIGN IS COMPLEX. AS RICHARD RUDD SAID IS a RICH AND COMPLEX;

IT INVOLVES A LOT OF DATA. THE SYSTEM IS A SYNTHESIS OF EASTERN AND WESTERN ASTROLOGY, THE CHINESE I'CHING, THE KABBALAH, THE HINDU CHAKRA SYSTEM AND QUANTUM .

I find some quiet time for meditation. The dawn just breaks. A cool breeze blows. Stars die out one by one. I do my left and right nostril breathing for balancing the flow of prana. I activate my chakras and feel the swirl of energy in the body, which aligns me to the universal swirl of the stars and constellation. I focus my attention to my senses. The smell of 'Michelia Camelia' wafts in. The grass feels soft under the feet. The bird songs, the koels, the parrots, the pidgeons, the squirrels, the crickets, the sparrows, and the far off cries of the peacocks, become an ensemble of beats, rhythms, and melodies, an orchestra of nature.

I begin with my **'anapanasati'** breathing. Next, concentrating on the 'agya' chakra, I try still my mind. Slowly the wild swings of the mind are pacified. The world outside dissolves. For fleeting moments there is a complete state of nothingness. Peace descends.

It is time for tea!

In the early hours of dawn, when the little birds sing their song,

An enchanted melody, a chorus of joy,

And you think, "Whoever taught them! Did they know it all along?"

The gentle breeze rustles among the leaves, a

magnificent tree, and you wonder how anyone could fit it into a seed,

Flowers of a hundred colours, sweetest fragrances, carrying tiny drops of nectar inside,

The buzzing bee, the gentle calf, the roaring lion, the elephant, the giraffe

Just who could it be, who fashioned all this!

The unsolved puzzle is 'who am I'.

I have never experienced a single thought independent of my living, functioning body to help produce it. There is no thinker without a brain and body, no seer without seeing, no hearer without hearing. The moment that thinking stops, this "thinker" vanishes altogether because there is no thinker at all. No seer. No hearer. There is only (the activities of) thinking, seeing, hearing, and so on. There is no lurker behind the scenes, no experiencer sitting at an imaginary control panel in our minds or bodies.

There is no 'I'. We have a distorted vision of our holographic reality. And our individual self is the source of distortion. The only reality is a void, no 'you', no 'I'. Only one unified truth – the 'advait' truth.

In the manner of Ramana Maharishi, teachers like **Rupert Spira, Jeff Foster, Eckharte Tolle, Mooji. Pappaji, Sadhguru, speak of the same ultimate 'ADVAIT' truth.**

We are all spirits that have come for a purpose here.

The current Western world view established by the English philosopher, Hobbes is that the universe, the solar system and our bodies are machines. Our minds and bodies are all separate parts of the machine.

But we have now come to know that everything we see, touch or feel are vibrations. We are energy, we are vibrations, all parts of one reality-the universal consciosness, the unchanging energy of NOW.

Closing thoughts...

I realise that it is time to close the doors. My generation has grown old. All of us have our sons and daughters who are ready to wear the mantle. A new generation, a new age and new ideas are waiting to take over from us. It is time to pass on the baton!

When we pass through the day

With nothing much to say

What can we do*!*   ***Paul Anka, Closing Doors***

Life goes on, it is a continuous process. The pulse of life does not stop. He past stays as we move forward. The past memories tumble out at every step, and give us immense joy, and satisfaction.

My son and his fiancée, Lucile, a French/American girl, are in San Francisco, in separate research engagements. Siddhansh is in life sciences and Lucile in data bank management for drugs and medicines. They are getting married in November 2023.

I HAVE COME TO THE EÑD THE BOOK.

BUT THE STORY GOES ON.

THE START OF A NEW JOURNEY!

Siddhansh and Lucille

My Paintings: a glimpse

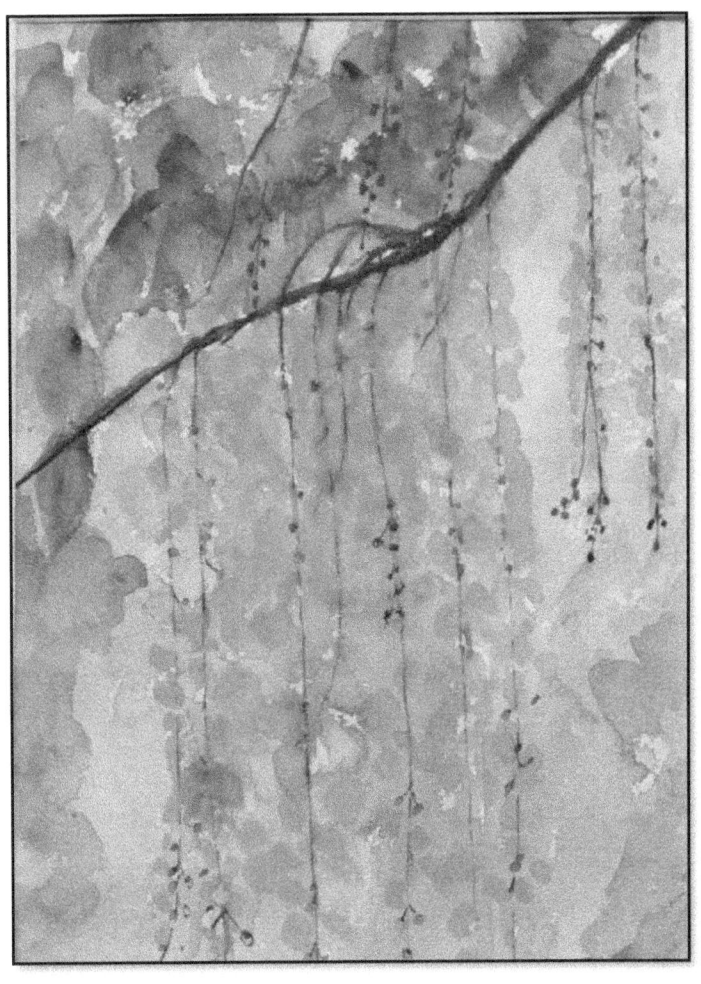

www.ingramcontent.com/pod-product-compliance
Lightning Source LLC
LaVergne TN
LVHW010333070526
838199LV00065B/5734